D1558613

CHILDREN
OF
VIETNAM

CHILDREN
OF
VIETNAM

*Betty Jean Lifton
and
Thomas C. Fox*

*Illustrated with photographs by
Thomas C. Fox*

Atheneum 1974 New York

TEXT COPYRIGHT © 1972 BY BETTY JEAN LIFTON AND THOMAS C. FOX
ILLUSTRATIONS COPYRIGHT © 1972 BY THOMAS C. FOX
ALL RIGHTS RESERVED
LIBRARY OF CONGRESS CATALOG CARD NUMBER 72-75274
ISBN 0-689-30056-5
PUBLISHED SIMULTANEOUSLY IN CANADA BY MC CLELLAND & STEWART LTD.
MANUFACTURED IN THE UNITED STATES OF AMERICA BY
HALLIDAY LITHOGRAPH CORPORATION,
WEST HANOVER, MASSACHUSETTS
FIRST PRINTING SEPTEMBER 1972
SECOND PRINTING AUGUST 1973
THIRD PRINTING FEBRUARY 1974

FOR
THE CHILDREN OF VIETNAM
AND
THE CHILDREN OF AMERICA

Contents

INTRODUCTION: CHILDREN OF THE DRAGON,
    THE FAIRY, AND THE WAR   2

TWO SISTERS OF CAN THO   6

A REFUGEE CHILD   13

ORPHANS   22

CHILD OF THE BACK STREETS OF SAIGON   32

STREET CHILDREN—THE "DUST OF LIFE"   40

A SAIGON HIPPIE   55

AN AMERASIAN BOY   62

THE WAR WOUNDED   71

A MONTAGNARD GIRL   83

A GIRL OF THE N L F   91

THE CHILDREN OF MY LAI   99

EPILOGUE   111

The shape of Vietnam has been likened to a starved sea horse.

A dragon fish.

Two baskets of rice supported by a long pole.

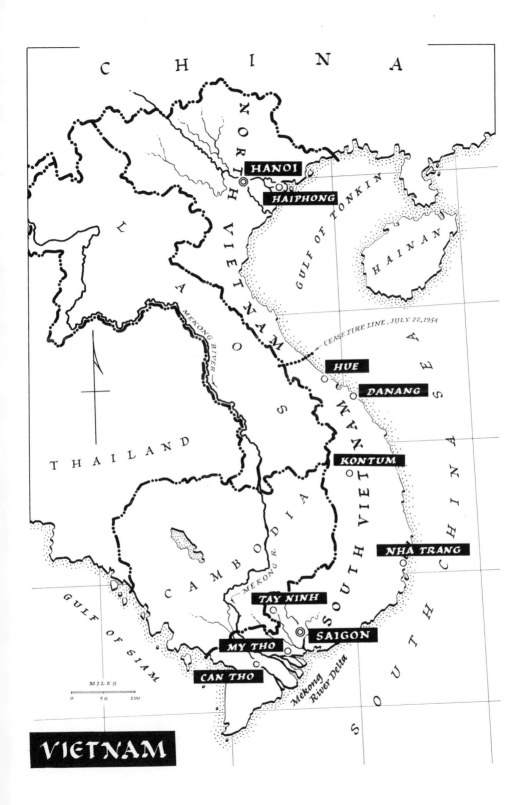

CHILDREN
OF
VIETNAM

INTRODUCTION: *Children of the Dragon, the Fairy, and the War*

Vietnam, I Hope You Feel Better

Vietnam, I hope you feel better, hope the war ends, hope you get the right government, hope our government lets you get the kind of government you want, hope there's peace there, hope people stop getting shot. I'm glad you have a one-day peace in Vietnam because of Christmas. I hope that you could have peace there all the time.

LARRY JACOBS, AGE SIX

The Heritage of Our Motherland

A thousand years slaves of the Chinese,
A hundred years dominated by the French,
Twenty years of civil war,
The heritage of our Motherland,
To leave for her children,
The heritage of our Motherland,
The sad country of Vietnam.

TRINH CONG SON

THE CHILDREN OF VIETNAM ARE SAID TO BE DESCENDED FROM A dragon and a fairy who divided their offspring and their country between them. This book is about the children of today who live once again in a divided Vietnam, in historical time. A time of war.

None of the children you will read about has ever known peace. The cycle of their lives is determined by troop movements and air raids, rather than the harvesting of crops. For them hunger, fear, and death are as regular as the seasons.

They are the children of war.

Peace has not come yet in early 1972 as we write. In these pages we hope to communicate some part of what we experienced when we went in search of the children in what is now South Vietnam. We hope we can capture these children: the gaiety they have somehow managed to retain. Their disarming spontaneity balanced by a dignified shyness. Their fantastic courage in the face of hardship and their resultant precociousness.

We have looked for these young people throughout the countryside, where most of the war is being fought. We have looked in the refugee camps, the orphanages, the hospitals, and in the city streets. We have looked in the homes of provincial and urban families whose daily routines seem unaffected by the conflict.

We have learned that the lives of all the children of Vietnam have been touched in one way or another by this war which has continued its demonic course for the past twenty-seven years. First as a struggle for liberation against the colonial French; and now as a civil war in which America has intervened militarily to bolster a series of unstable governments in the South against the nationalistically inspired Communist government of the late Ho Chi Minh in the North.

Some of the children we have written about have grown up in broken homes while their fathers were in the armies of one side or the other. Some have left home to live on the streets. Some have lost their limbs in the bombings. Some have been scarred emotionally from watching their villages burn, their parents die. Some may no longer be alive.

Of course, the Vietnam War is not unique in its sacrifice of the young. Think of the youthful victims in the violent twentieth century alone. Those who died in World War I. The children who perished in the fire bombings of the great cities of Europe and in the gas chambers of Auschwitz, Dachau, and Bergen-Belsen in World War II. Think of the A-bombed children of Hiroshima and Nagasaki. Think of the children of Korea.

Yes, think.

The Vietnam War is unique in other ways, though. It is a war in which there are no front lines—where the whole country is a battlefield. Where anything that moves is the enemy.

And children move.

It is a war where one side uses the ground tactics of guerrilla warfare and the other the advanced technology of an air war. Where American planes bomb the very villages they are supposedly defending in the hope of finding the elusive enemy.

They often find the children.

It is a war in which people argue over statistics like whether a quarter million or a million children have been killed or wounded.

Who can count all the dead?

This book has come out of our own experiences as journalists in

Vietnam. One of us, a writer in the children's field, has traveled there twice: in 1954 after the French had been defeated by the troops of Ho Chi Minh, and again in the summer of 1967 when America was deeply committed to the war. The other has lived for a year and a half as an International Volunteer Services worker among the destitute peasants in a refugee camp, and now, married to a Vietnamese social worker, is reporting for *The New York Times*.

In a sense we are witnesses.

And as such, we must tell what we have seen.

BETTY JEAN LIFTON
THOMAS C. FOX
New York—Saigon

Two Sisters of Can Tho

I Shall Go Visiting

When my land has peace
I shall go visiting,
I shall go visiting
Along a road with many foxholes.
When my land is no longer at war
I shall visit the green graves of my friends;
When my land has peace
I shall go visiting
I shall go visiting
Over bridges crushed by mines,
Go visiting
Bunkers of bayonets and pungi sticks;
When my people are no longer killing each other
The children will sing children's songs
Outside on the street.

TRINH CONG SON

IT HAS LONG BEEN A TRADITION IN VIETNAM FOR PARENTS TO choose their children's names with great care. The proper one, some believe, can bring good fortune to the family. A boy called Ai Quoc ("Patriot") will probably love his country. (Ho Chi Minh adopted this name as an alias during his years in exile.) A girl called Hoa ("Flower") will probably grow to be gentle and lovely. So, too, will one called Spring Flower or Golden Mountain. All of the choices reveal the deeply romantic nature of the Vietnamese.

Today many names carry more hope within them than a child can carry within his heart.

Ngoc Tram ("Precious Hairpin"), age six, and her five-year-old sister, Ngoc Truc ("Precious Bamboo"), are two city children still living with the grace their names imply. Born in Can Tho, a provincial capital in the fertile, rice-producing Mekong River Delta, they have missed the immediate impact of the war being waged in the countryside. Unlike the thousands of refugees who are crowded into miserable one-room shanties throughout the town, Tram and Truc are sheltered behind the high garden walls of their spacious brick home, which has been in the family for the past half century. Their father, a lawyer, has an office there, and their maternal grandparents live with them.

The sisters' home stood intact even during the massive Tet offensive in 1968, when the Viet Cong and the North Vietnamese brought the battle into the cities. Heavy street fighting and bombing occurred in Can Tho then, but not in their section. And although

7

the markets and stores were closed down for nearly a week, the girls' family had enough rice and fish to last them through the emergency.

Now the sisters are just entering the first grade of a local private school. Learning is highly valued in this old culture, and their grandmother has spent many hours teaching them at home. Already they can read simple Vietnamese animal fables and stories about the nobility of past ages.

However, in keeping with the customs of well-bred girls, they do not flaunt their knowledge, but rather cultivate a seemingly natural reticence. Tram is so shy in school that her younger sister, Truc, must answer questions for her. Tram whispers her reply to Truc who relays it to the teacher. Since they share the same class, the system works well.

On Sundays the sisters look forward to visiting relatives in a village about five miles from Can Tho. But since their family is among the South's million and a half Catholics, they must wait patiently for their parents to return from Mass. Only then can they jump into the family car and move quickly through the city and out into the lush green of the tropics.

By now Tram and Truc take for granted the American air base at Binh Thuy, which they must pass. This unnatural growth sits wrapped like so much of the countryside in miles and miles of metal coil: barbed wire around the mournful accretion of Quonset huts, around the brilliant green of the rice paddies, around fields in which the large white tombstones of the ancestors sprout like giant toadstools, around the ever-present refugee camps. Barbed wire that stops the elusive Viet Cong no more effectively than do bombs or artillery fire.

Beyond the base with its convoys of trucks stirring up dust and belching black clouds of exhaust fumes that blind the eyes and parch the throat, the road is quiet again. Only a few Hondas and cars follow its winding course through the fertile paddies. The peasants are too busy planting to look up from their work. The girls glimpse neat thatched huts nestling in mango and palm trees. A woman in a doorway is nursing her baby; a water buffalo swats flies with its tail as it lounges in the shade of a banana tree.

This tranquil scene soon dissolves into a more ominous one: their car passes over a bridge guarded by two armored tanks. Vietnamese soldiers carrying M-16 rifles talk together, bored by their duty. A large red and yellow sign strung out boldly over their heads reads:

A COALITION GOVERNMENT IS SUICIDE. The words mean little to
the girls who have become used to seeing such warnings everywhere.

At last they arrive at their uncle's house. The girls run off
eagerly into the wooded groves that surround it, while their father
lingers behind to speak with his brother.

The paths are narrow. Tram stumbles over a fallen branch. Truc
follows quickly, afraid of being left behind. The sisters are fas-
cinated by the woods but believe that spirits live in certain trees.
"Chu Ba! Chu Ba!" (Third Uncle) they cry out with relief as they
see a familiar figure working in a rice field. He turns and waves.

By now their father has joined them and they continue together
through the thick branches that cut them off from the heat of the
afternoon sun. Joyfully, they make their way through the maze of
mangoes, coconut palms, jackfruit, and grapefruit trees, stopping
only to pick the flowers that are growing everywhere.

Many South Vietnamese believe the lush vegetation of the Delta
accounts for their personality. They recognize that they are
slower and more easygoing than Northerners, who must work hard
for their rice in the harsher climate. But, although admittedly less
ambitious, they pride themselves on being more straightforward
and honest.

Tram and Truc's family land has had a life nearly as charmed as
their own. It has never been a battlefield. Defoliants fell on the
fields on two occasions, but the doses were relatively light. Only
one uncle has been lost in the war, although many of their cousins
have been conscripted into both armies.

Even among the Catholics, who are mainly anti-Communist,
decisions as to which side to join depend most often on practical
matters, such as whether government forces or the Viet Cong con-
trol the village when a boy turns eighteen. But no matter who fights

where, blood ties run deeper than political differences. Each time Tet, the Vietnamese New Year, rolls around, all the men in Tram and Truc's extended family sit down and eat and drink and worship at the ancestral tombs together.

The girls watch the sky anxiously as the sun begins to approach the tops of the distant palm trees. They know it is time to set off for Can Tho. Folding their arms, an elbow in each hand, they give the traditonal bow to their uncle, and everyone piles back into the car.

When they arrive back home, Tram and Truc's most urgent concern is how best to use the flowers they picked and packed away in their baskets. Some will be painted or pasted on paper for decorations; others will be made into necklaces and bracelets. The largest flowers will be given to their grandparents as souvenirs of their trip.

On Sunday nights the girls like to watch the traditional Vietnamese plays broadcast on TV from Saigon. Theirs is the first generation to see such wonders coming from a small box. They will tell you without hesitation that when they grow up they want to become television stars. Their father laughs uncomfortably, knowing that members of their family do not become entertainers.

Tonight the play is the story of the Trung sisters who lived nearly two thousand years ago. Sometimes referred to as the Joans of Arc of Vietnam, they were also of high birth. But when the husband of Trung Trac, the older sister, was executed by the brutal Chinese occupation army, the sisters raised their own troops and drove the enemy out. Trung Trac was proclaimed queen of the land, which found itself for the first time free of foreign domination.

However, the victory was short-lived. Three years later, in 43, A.D., the Chinese sent more soldiers to defeat the queen's men. Rather than surrender, the Trung sisters drowned themselves in a river. Vietnam was ruled by China for the next thousand years, but it never forgot the valor of those two women. Even today both North and South claim them as national heroines, and both have named streets after them.

Tram and Truc watch with large eyes as the glorious Trung sisters struggle valiantly on television before them. But it is doubtful either child will ever become an actress or a Vietnamese heroine. It is more likely they will both grow to be wives and mothers like the generations before them.

Yet the Vietnamese say the fates are never predictable. And who can know what will someday be the destiny of these two sisters of Can Tho?

A Refugee Child

"What, oh, what is the use of war? Why can't people live peacefully together? Why all this destruction? . . . There's in people simply an urge to destroy, an urge to kill, to murder and rage, and until all mankind, without exception, undergoes a great change, wars will be waged, everything that has been built up, cultivated, and grown will be destroyed and disfigured, after which mankind will have to begin all over again."

ANNE FRANK, AGE FOURTEEN
The Diary of a Young Girl

"To take a leaf from Mao Tse-tung's *Red Book,* we've got to deprive the fish of the sea to swim in. . . . We're going to dig Vietnam up by the rice roots and replant it, if necessary, until their infrastructure is totally destroyed. Remove the people from the guerrillas, turn the area into a free-fire zone and shoot anything that moves."

AMERICAN ARMY MAJOR
BINH DINH PROVINCE
Crimes of War

"Once upon a time, from this spot, one could see coconut and bamboo trees growing in a huge rice field. This was my hamlet. Now there is only bare ground. All the images of the old days have vanished. . . . Everything had gone. Like someone who had lost his soul, I wanted to scream out my own inability to preserve what had been left to me by my ancestors."

NGOC KY
"A Visit to My Village"
Between Two Fires

THIRTEEN-YEAR-OLD NGUYEN VAN TAM IS A REFUGEE. HE IS, IN fact, just one of at least six million Vietnamese who have been uprooted during the past six years. Now he lives with his mother and two younger sisters behind barbed wire in what is known as a refugee camp.

The war has taken the meaning out of words, just as it has taken the meaning out of Tam's life. Webster's dictionary defines a refugee as one who flees to safety. Yet Tam and his family were forced to leave their hamlet in Quang Nam province three years ago when American airplanes dropped leaflets designating the area a "free-fire zone." They were warned that they had twenty-four hours to vacate before anything left moving would be considered an open target.

Tam is old enough to remember his village life, something his two younger sisters can hardly do. "I used to take the water buffalo out to graze when the sun rose in the morning. It was fun to wake up. And cool then. As the sun kept rising in the sky, it became too hot for the buffaloes to eat. Then I would return home and have lunch with my parents and sisters. In the afternoons, after siesta, I played with my friends. We liked to hide and climb the coconut palms."

Tam remembers, too, the banana and jackfruit trees that used to shade his house, and the friendly herons who followed the good-natured buffaloes to eat the insects off their backs.

But he also remembers less pleasant things. He speaks with fright about B-52 strikes in the mountains and silver jets that strafed the paths where his buffaloes grazed.

"The airplanes bombed most often in the afternoons. Usually when we heard them coming we ran into the shelter under our house. But if we were far from the shelter, we knew it was safer not to move. The planes do not see you if you stay still."

The bombs and artillery shells were so alien to Tam that he had no way of understanding where they came from or why they were firing on him. Like all Vietnamese children, his knowledge of the world had been absorbed from the three pillars of Vietnamese thought—mystic Taoism, Confucian order, and Buddhist resignation. He knew that little in life can be changed and that he must accept things as they are. But though he had been taught to respect nature, he had also been told not to be defeated by it.

"The floods cannot be stopped, yet they can be resisted," his father would say.

So, too, with American technology. The bombs could not be stopped, but they could be resisted. The planes and the Americans, like the floods and other natural disasters, would not last forever.

Tam cannot guess how many bombs were dropped on his village. But he does remember one very well—the one that killed his father.

"My father was a farmer—a good farmer. We did not own the land, but he knew it better than the landlord. He showed me how to plant the rice and take care of the chickens and pigs. We talked together about everything. I loved him very much.

"It was my father who told me not to move when the planes came. If there was time before they arrived, he said, I should lie down in a ditch until the bombs stopped falling and the guns stopped shooting.

"I was in the shelter the afternoon my father was killed in the rice field. The planes came suddenly and I know he did not run. But they saw him anyway. I heard the explosions that got him. They should not have killed my father. He was a good man.''

A few days after his father's death, American soldiers entered Tam's village.

"They looked very big. They carried large guns, and their noses were very long. They spoke, but none of us understood what they were saying. I was afraid, but my mother said I must not hide. That I must not show my fear.

"That day some Americans came into our house. They pointed to the road and said we must all leave. My mother cried. They took matches and burned our house. Then they shot our buffaloes." Tam pauses before adding, "Then we began to walk to the refugee camp outside Danang to find shelter and food."

Danang is the second largest city in Vietnam. It is also the site of one of the biggest American air bases in the country. Many of the refugee camps are located near such bases to provide jobs for the peasants and cheap, unskilled labor for the military.

Tam and his family found themselves resettled in the Hoa Khanh camp along with forty thousand other refugees. It was only fifteen miles from their former home, but unlike anything they had ever known. Nothing but small cactus plants grew around them on the dry, barren soil. Tam's uncle helped them build a one-room shack from the wood they gathered from the air base. The government provided tin for the roof, but there was no relief from the relentless heat. The metal made their dwelling ovenlike in the tropical sun. The cool breezes, which Vietnamese believe carried good spirits and health through the old thatched structures, could not pass through the inhospitable tin.

For the first six months, like all refugees who chose to live in a camp, Tam and his family received a limited amount of rice and piasters from the South Vietnamese government. But after that period they were considered resettled even though they still had no

means of support. No one seemed concerned that a farmer could not farm when he had no land. No one cared that none of them had the equipment to fish in the coastal waters.

Tam does not know that he and the other villagers were moved from their fertile inland rice fields to the unarable sands along the coast so that they and their crops would be inaccessible to the Viet Cong guerrillas. But he knows that everyone has somehow changed.

In the past his neighbors did not look upon themselves as individuals but rather as part of a rice-growing hamlet. Now those who once cooperated in planting and harvesting, who shared buffaloes and plows and aided each other in time of need, are fighting for the few jobs available on the army base or in the American construction company.

The economic hardships of those who live in the Hoa Khanh camp are only exceeded by the spiritual agony they suffer, an agony little understood by foreigners. For the peasants have been torn away from the spiritual centers of their lives—their ancestral

graves. When they cannot make offerings to their ancestors, their precious link with the world of the spirits is severed. They must bear the torment of knowing that their beloved dead may wander aimlessly in limbo because of their neglect, and that they too may suffer such a fate.

Tam does not dwell now upon the ancestors; he is too busy taking on man-sized responsibilities for his little family. There are no "older brothers" in the camp to guide him, for the armies of the government or the Viet Cong have taken them, or they have been killed, like his father. In this setting where money far exceeds age in importance, the old have lost the authority they once held. The younger children run unattended through the compound. They have the distended stomachs and skin ailments that malnutrition brings on. Many of their older sisters have disappeared into the glittering world of the bars of Danang, where they can earn money as prostitutes. Mothers look for any menial work they can find.

At first Tam's mother was able to find some work at the nearby military base, but when the American troops began to be withdrawn in sizable numbers, jobs like hers were cut back. Now she goes out each morning gathering firewood to sell for thirty cents a day on the local market.

Tam and his sister no longer can afford to eat meat, and even some fish is beginning to be too expensive for them. Their usual diet now is crushed shrimp, rice and salt. Like the other refugees, they often go to sleep hungry.

Yet Tam is fortunate. He has been able to resist the epidemics of polio, measles, cholera, and even the plague, which take the very young and the very old. And he has made friends with a Filipino social worker who started a poultry project in the camp. For taking care of the chickens in the morning, he gets a simple lunch each day. However, because of his job, Tam cannot attend the makeshift school also set up for the refugees. His younger sister is learning to read and write her name there, something he still cannot do.

"When I am older," he says wistfully, "I want to be a mechanic."

"You do not want to return to your village?"

He is startled by the question, as if temporarily jolted out of the immediate futility of his life. "Oh, yes, when the Americans leave, we will all return to our villages," he says brightly.

Then he pauses. "When will the Americans leave?"

Perhaps Tam suspects that even when the war ends and the Americans leave, the children will not return with their parents to the villages. Many of them no longer exist, having been razed in the bombings and search-and-destroy missions. Many of the fields have been ruined with herbicides. It may take years to coax the soil back into the fertility of the past.

It will take millions of dollars to rebuild the houses, repair the dikes, buy equipment for farming and livestock. The old will be too weak to do the heavy work that will be necessary in the fields. Most of the able-bodied men will have been killed or crippled. And some of the young who have tasted the ways of urban life may not want to return to rural living.

The fabric of village life has been severely torn. It will take generations to mend, and even then its texture can never be the same.

Tam cannot write a diary of longing and waiting as did Anne Frank during the Second World War, for he is illiterate. But his life behind barbed wire and his loss of the past are written in his heart.

Whom will he accuse? The Americans? The Viet Cong? The South Vietnamese government? He does not think of that.

"When will peace come?" he asks.

He no longer expects an answer.

Orphans

I Met You at the Orphanage Yard

Your sad eyes
overflowed with
loneliness
and pain.
You saw me.
You turned your face away.
Your hands drew circles,
circles
on the dusty ground.

I dared not ask you
where your father
and your mother were.
I dared not open up your wounds.
I only wished to sit with you
a moment
saying a word or two.

THICH NHAT HANH
The Cry of Vietnam

UNTIL RECENTLY AN ORPHANAGE WAS AN ALIEN CONCEPT IN Vietnam. The family-oriented culture knew how to take care of its young: if something happened to a parent, the nearest relative took the children in. However, now, after so many years of a war in which many villages have been totally destroyed and whole populations forcibly removed from their ancestral lands, children have been either orphaned or separated from their kin.

Officially there are one hundred and twenty registered orphanages in South Vietnam, caring for about nineteen thousand children. There is no way of knowing how many hundreds of unregistered ones exist, but it is safe to say that at least a hundred thousand children have been separated from their families. Some are real orphans; some have one parent somewhere with whom they may eventually be reunited. Many of the infants have been abandoned because their parents could no longer care for them.

A society's degradation is most clearly revealed when it begins abandoning its young. Mothers in Vietnam leave their ailing newborn infants by an orphanage or hospital gate with the desperate hope that they will have a better chance for survival. But many of these children are so weakened by malnutrition by the time they are found, they are difficult to save.

All orphanages lack adequate personnel and medical facilities. Those which are registered receive monthly payments from the Vietnamese Ministry of Social Welfare amounting to $1.50 a child, which is about one eighth of their operating expenses.

CARE, Catholic Relief Services, and United States Army units have in the past tried to supplement this with clothes, flour, meat, and cooking oil. But with the American withdrawal and the gradual cutback of voluntary agencies, the orphanages' meager subsistence level is being threatened. Many of the smaller ones are being forced to close down.

Only a minimal number of children have been adopted by American or European families because of the bureaucratic red tape set up by the South Vietnamese government. It takes a year for a child to get an exit visa. Since there must be verification that the parents are dead or written permission from the family letting the child leave the country, most of the orphans fail to qualify. Village records have been burned with the houses, and the whereabouts of relatives are usually unknown.

Unless sufficient funds are allocated for the orphans, there is little hope at all for their future. Many of the older children are either crippled by polio or suffering from eye and ear diseases as well as T.B. and other ailments their frail bodies cannot resist. To walk past row upon row of emaciated babies in Vietnam's institutions is to know that most of them will not be alive the following month and that there will be others to take their place. The mortality rate among infants is ninety per cent in many orphanages.

A few Westerners who have tried waiting out the long, complicated adoption procedures have learned this painfully; babies they had carefully chosen have died of malnutrition before the paperwork was completed.

KHAN

Khan was one of the lucky babies. A few months after her birth she was left near death on the doorsteps of a Saigon hospital, suffering from extreme malnutrition. She was taken immediately to Caritas, a Catholic social center set up especially for the young who might otherwise die of starvation. Hospitals and orphanages are eager to send their infants there, where they receive special diets to help them develop normally. But the Caritas school for the young, run by two Catholic nuns and nineteen women social workers, is equipped to care for only one hundred children at a time.

Khan has been at Caritas two years. She is a quiet child, developing slowly, almost as if she is reluctant to continue the struggle for life that she nearly lost. She plays apart from the other children, mostly observing, seldom trying to express her own thoughts. Perhaps it is her fragility in a country where only the strongest can survive that has made her a favorite among the staff.

The Sisters follow an organized schedule. Most of the children are under three, and eat, sleep, and play according to their particular age group. In the mornings they are taken outside to a yard next to the center. After lunch there is a siesta until three, and then play until dinner. Bedtime is at eight.

Most of the children have never seen a toy. Since they are not used to playing with objects, they crawl about the floors, improvising what activities they can. They have the apathy of those who have grown to expect little and so withdraw into their own private worlds.

Occasionally a child at Caritas is adopted by a wealthy Vietnamese or by a European or American family. But as the government discourages adoptions, it is the exception for them to go abroad.

It is possible that Khan's mother is still alive. Should she show up at the hospital where she left her child, she would be directed to Caritas. The Sisters feel that it is unlikely this will happen.

Since children only stay at Caritas for four to six months, Khan has been there longer than anyone. The Sisters admit that eventually she too must move on to a regular orphanage. As if she understands this, Khan clings to her helplessness just as she clings to the staff. She still cannot eat by herself very well, and will not go to the toilet alone. Something in her knows that to become self-sufficient might be to lose the only affection she has ever known.

But sentiment is a luxury in a country where death and destruction are part of everyday life. Khan, like the others before her, will have to move on to make room for abandoned newborns even more helpless than she.

A BUDDHIST ORPHANAGE

Buddhist orphanages are a new phenomenon in Vietnam, and noticeably poorer than the Catholic ones. During the early years of the war, Americans felt they could "trust" the Catholics more than the Buddhists, who were for the most part anti-government and considered "militant." Then, too, with Catholic and Protestant chaplains as the link, it was easier to funnel American assistance into the Catholic orphanages. Catholics were also more experienced in running such organizations than the Buddhists, who entered the field of social welfare only in the middle sixties as part of a new period called engaged Buddhism.

South of Saigon, where the city abruptly dissolves into the Delta, there is a small orphanage started by some Buddhist nuns in 1964. It was named after Dieu Quang, the nun who immolated herself with fire to protest the regime of Ngo Dinh Diem.

In front of the orphanage stands the tall statue of Quan An, the compassionate protectress of children. According to Buddhist legend, Quan An was a beautiful young woman who sacrificed her own life to beg in the streets for an abandoned baby. Now she stands mournfully watching over the one hundred and thirty homeless children in her keeping.

With those two strong women as spiritual guides, one from the mythological past and the other from the stormy historical present, the young orphans, who range in age from two weeks to fifteen years, go through their daily routines in a world devoid of men. They are supervised by ten nuns and twenty female laborers, who help with everything from bathing the children to selling soy sauce to support the orphanage. Isolated, as most orphans are, from the rest of society, they look forward to riding into Saigon once a month to visit an An Quang Pagoda. But even then they must usually stay in the bus, for there are too many of them for their attendants to keep track of.

Each year the Dieu Quang has expanded. "As long as the war lasts, our numbers will increase," said a nun. "But one of the tragedies of life in an orphanage is that the children accept being here as normal. They do not know they really *should* have parents."

Like most Buddhist orphanages, the Dieu Quang no longer allows anyone to adopt their children. The nuns were shocked to discover that the children were being used as servants by wealthy Vietnamese families. And they do not want to lose their children to foreigners who would most probably not bring them up as Buddhists.

Visitors are not too common, and so the orphans seldom have a chance to talk to adults from the outside world. Rarely do they think into the future or the past, but live only in their immediate daily routine. Though the Sisters work hard to give their charges adequate care, they admit there is no way a child can be given the individual attention he or she needs.

TUYET

Huynh Thien Tuyet, a thirteen-year-old girl, is one of the few children who remembers anything at all about her early life. She came to the orphanage seven years ago from a tiny village in the Delta.

"My mother died when I was very small," she recalls. "Then my father tried to take care of my younger brother and me. We were very poor. He would send us off to my uncle sometimes when he did not have enough food."

Tuyet speaks of being afraid of the planes that flew over the fields daily, and of how friends came in to help whenever her father had to go away to fight for a week or two.

"One day when we were at home, my uncle came to tell us that my father had been killed fighting somewhere near our village. He brought us to this orphanage and said that life would be happy here.

"At first I cried a lot, but after a while I found that I was no longer sad. I could eat and play with the other children. I could go to school right here on the grounds. That's what I like to do best. Now that I am older, I can watch my younger brother. I also help the Sisters prepare meals and give the little children baths."

Although no one mentions it, the location of her village and the circumstances of her father's death suggest that Tuyet's was a Viet Cong family. But the Buddhists are not concerned about the political backgrounds of their children, only their spiritual future.

HUNG

Hung, who has been at the Dieu Quang orphanage for four years, is too young to remember his past. He says he is nine, but the nuns believe he is only seven. Asked where his home is, he replies shyly, "Here." Asked where his parents are, he says, "Buried."

He speaks of his brothers and sisters, but the nuns say he is referring to the other orphans. No one seems to know where he came from, but it seems certain his parents are not living.

Hung wears the same haircut as the other boys—a long bang and shaven head. It is similar to the hairdo of young children who enter the pagoda to become monks. But the orphans are not forced to become monks or even Buddhists. The only requirement is that they pray in the lotus position for fifteen minutes to a half-hour every evening after they finish dinner. During the day they study at the orphanage school from seven thirty to eleven in the morning

and then from three thirty to five in the afternoon.

Hung does not ask questions about his origins yet. "It is usually the ten-year-olds who begin to wonder about their parents," a nun explains. "That's the age they first realize their lives are not like the other Vietnamese."

Until he is ten, Hung will continue to live together with all the children in his age group, sleeping and bathing with them. After that he and the other boys will be separated from the girls. Since the young are not taught to regard sex as evil or even strange, they consider it quite natural to live together now as brothers and sisters in their large parentless family.

When they are not in school, the children are free to play on the open fields that are part of the orphanage's property, but no one is allowed to leave without permission. This is no problem, for there is simply no place else to go.

Child of the Back Streets
of Saigon

Once you were so little.
Father fed you rice. Mother made you clothes.
Your teacher gave you words. Now you've grown.
How will you fulfill our hopes?

VIETNAMESE FOLK SONG

NINE-YEAR-OLD UT IS GROWING UP IN SAIGON ON A CROWDED BACK alley that most foreigners never see. Like many of the three million Vietnamese who populate this teeming capital, she knows little more about it than the twisting maze of pathways where she plays.

Only once has Ut glimpsed the Saigon that foreigners know. The Saigon of luxury hotels, expensive French and Chinese restaurants, gaudy nightclubs and bars. The Saigon that the French had designed as their "Paris of the East," with wide, tree-lined boulevards and spacious, pastel houses to remind them of home during their colonial period. The Saigon whose streets are now filled with beggars, homeless children, and prostitutes; whose lawns are planted with sandbags and bordered with barbed wire.

Since that day when she drove through the city with her father, Ut's world has again closed quietly upon itself. Her narrow, unpaved road is hardly any wider than the door of the frame home in which she lives with her nine brothers and sisters, as well as the children and husbands of her three oldest sisters. Although fighting rages sporadically in the nearby countryside, her life is unaffected by it. The sound of artillery in the distance every night is no more threatening than the evening rain upon the roof during the monsoon season. She doesn't bother to look up anymore when a low-flying helicopter passes overhead on its way to or from a military mission.

The family struggles continually to maintain a subsistence level in the constantly rising inflation of the city. Her father, a chauffeur for a top official in the Ministry of Labor, works every day from seven in the morning to six in the evening to earn a modest eighty-four dollars monthly. With this and her mother's earnings at the local market, they can live frugally while owning a television and even the most coveted of all household luxuries, an electric fan.

Ut's father's life reflects the constantly changing fortunes of his country. A native of North Vietnam, he was driving for the French when the Japanese took over the country in World War II. He did not refuse the offer of a Japanese officer to go to Saigon.

"For that money I'd drive for anyone," he says. "A poor man goes where the money's most." He might have added that one foreigner is the same as another.

Not long after his arrival in Saigon, he met Ut's mother, married, moved into her neighborhood, and took on her clan as his own.

Ut, which means "the smallest," is the youngest daughter in the family, but she has a still younger brother. Vietnamese refer to their children by numerals. It is convenient in their large families, and confuses any evil spirits that might do harm, especially to the first-born. For this reason the oldest child in the South is number two, not one. The rest follow in numerical order. By doing this, the parents can also be sure they will not offend an older relative who might have the same given name.

Ut's father does not remember what he originally called all his children. Counting slowly on his fingers while closing his eyes, he is unable to get past the fourth before losing track.

"If I look at their I.D. cards, I could tell you," he says with a broad grin.

Ut's life follows a simple routine. She gets up every morning at seven to get ready for school, which is just down the road. Her mother and older sisters have already risen at five to go to the cen-

tral fish market where they buy fish to sell at their own small market.

Like the other young children in the family, Ut does not eat breakfast at home but spends five cents for sugar rice, which is sold near her school. Her father and older brothers eat *pho,* a hot soup made of egg noodles and beef, which they also purchase from a street vendor.

Ut's classmates in the third grade are all from the poorer families on the alley. The wealthier households send their offspring to private or larger public schools several blocks away.

"I am second in my class in words and numbers," Ut says proudly.

Yet her future as far as education goes is not very promising. When she finishes the sixth grade, she must also begin selling fish.

If her morning classes let out early, Ut runs to the market at the end of the alley to walk home with her mother and sisters. Her mother then cooks lunch for the family. After the meal, Ut slips off her plastic sandals and folds herself into a low-slung hammock with a few of the younger children for the daily two-hour siesta. If the hammock is full before she gets there, she'll climb into a mosquito net that hangs over one of the wooden beds in the rear room of the house. But always she'll be snuggling next to another warm body as she drifts off to sleep.

Americans have tried to dispense with the siesta by making their Vietnamese employees return from lunch in the early afternoon. But even the war is known to stop in the hot midday sun for a brief rest.

In the late afternoon Ut stays at home and watches her younger brother and nieces and nephews. In Vietnamese families the responsibility of caring for the children is the task of the children themselves. Each is directly responsible for the one younger than he. It is not uncommon for Ut to carry her brother around on her hip for hours at a time.

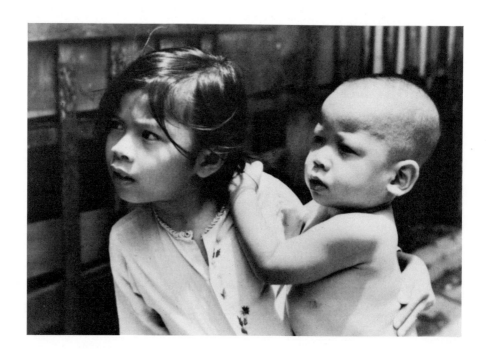

Ut often bathes the little ones while her mother and older sisters are doing the family washing. Unlike their neighbors, who must walk to the water taps attached to the larger houses, they are fortunate to have a pipe that connects them to the main line. A simple turn of the faucet and the water falls into a large pottery jar where it is warmed by the heat of the afternoon sun. Ut scoops it out with an aluminum bucket cut from an old American bombshell and fills a large plastic tub. Then, squatting next to her brother, she splashes the water over his body, cooling and cleaning him at the same time.

Outside in the alley, Ut puts her brother down to play a version of Scissors, Paper, Stone, or a game like hopscotch. The boys have their own diversions. They play marbles when they are available, or match coins against each other to see who can get the most.

Ut's father comes home by six-thirty on the French motorized bike he bought secondhand to take himself to and from work.

Actually his job is not too strenuous. Most of his time is spent just waiting alone inside the $20,000 Mercedes his employer uses. Saigon government officials seem to have an affinity for expensive cars. Occasionally he runs errands for his boss and gives the car a daily wash outside the Ministry of Labor.

While the children wait for their father, Ut's oldest brother plays records on an old family phonograph. He likes Hung Cuong, a popular Vietnamese singer, best. Her sisters, however, prefer Western music. Their collection includes Nancy Sinatra, the Ventures, the Byrds, and the Rolling Stones.

The family gathers for dinner in the kitchen, squatting together on the cement floor. Ut's mother has prepared rice, vegetables, and fish over the two small kerosene stoves that Ut helped her light with old newspapers. Ut has also cooked the rice, a task girls learn to do at an early age.

In the evening everyone watches TV on the Japanese set, which they paid for over a period of two years in monthly installments. Some of the poorest families in Saigon are able to buy TV's inexpensively, since the prices are subsidized by American aid. Ut's father puts his meager savings into such consumer commodities because he knows that the value of the piaster, which has fallen steadily over the past five years, will continue to fluctuate. Wealthy Vietnamese often turn their piasters into United States dollars on the black market and send them to banks in Hong Kong and Switzerland.

The television programs in Ut's house, like the music, are a mixture of East and West. The English-speaking Armed Forces Television begins telecasting at two in the afternoon. At seven in the evening the Vietnamese channel comes on. Ut's father always watches the news at seven-thirty. And then the family argument begins as to what will be on—the Vietnamese shows which Ut prefers, or the American westerns her brothers like because they have more action.

By ten in the evening the children are falling asleep, although the television may be blaring out "Combat," "Wild, Wild West," "Mission Impossible," or "Gunsmoke." By eleven, when the channels sign off, the little ones are marched off to their beds, mats, and hammocks by their parents. Each married sister's family has its own mosquito netting to separate it from the others. Ut and her family all share one room.

Does Ut dream sometimes of the day she glimpsed the wonders of that other Saigon? Does she remember the splendors she saw, or the guards with bayonets pointing from the doorways of government buildings and military barracks? Does she worry that her brothers will soon be old enough to go to war?

Or are her dreams more simple? Of a friend in school? Of the day when she will be married like her sisters and have children of her own?

As yet the harsher realities of Saigon need not intrude into Ut's dreams. She can lie cozily intertwined with the bodies of her brothers and sisters, safe in the comfort of her mother's words: "We do not ask to be rich. We ask only that our family gather together at night and sleep together in peace."

Street Children—
The "Dust of Life"

If only the children could have had the stars, the flowers and the butterflies, instead of the war.

PHUONG TRIEU
"The School on the Front Line"
Between Two Fires

War has always produced many innocent victims, but perhaps the most neglected are the countless waifs who appear on the city streets of an uprooted society. Homeless, displaced, betrayed by an adult community that often exploits them for its own purposes, they learn to survive in the streets much as soldiers learn to survive in the jungles.

Following the Bolshevik revolution, bands of what were officially called Wild Children roamed about the Russian countryside terrorizing the people. Not long after the atomic bomb fell in Hiroshima, thousands of orphans congregated at the railroad station, hustling, competing, taking part in black marketeering and prostitution. And now in Vietnam one finds tens of thousands of homeless youngsters staking out territory in the hostile, lonely streets.

Instead of "Wild Children," these young Vietnamese are called Bui Doi, the "Dust of Life," for they live like dust on the road, wandering as the wind takes them, being swept up from time to time by the city police, having no value to anyone.

Most of these children have been separated from their families by dislocation or death; some are runaways from refugee centers, orphanages, or their own fatherless homes. They live by their wits as shoeshine boys, pimps, pickpockets, and beggars. One recognizes them by their tattered short pants, soiled shirts, and dirt-smudged faces. One finds them sleeping in doorways, stealing parts from unguarded Honda motorbikes, or hustling American GI's.

41

There are very few girls among them.

Ranging in years from five to eighteen, the age at which they are picked up by police and forced into the South Vietnamese army, they group together in small bands. Outwardly they appear confident and aggressive, but inwardly they are loners, alienated from even their close friends.

The smallest, often carrying infant brothers or sisters in their arms, hang around downtown commercial areas, where begging or stealing is most profitable. Many an American soldier or civilian has had the experience of suddenly finding himself surrounded by these "innocent" little ones, their short arms outstretched, their lean bodies playfully jostling into his. Too late he discovers that his pockets have been emptied. The children scatter like a flock of birds into the crowds to spend the money on candy, movies, or whatever else they crave at the moment.

When the youngest lose their "cute" looks, they usually become shoeshine boys. From eleven to fifteen years of age, they often attempt to make an honest living by shining the huge boots of foreign soldiers. They hang out at theaters, enlisted men's clubs, and bars. Some of them just wander about with their little shoeshine kits, almost like survival kits in that they are the one possession that gives the boys a way to earn something for food each day. They are proud of their special techniques, such as melting the polish with a match onto the toe of the boot to make it easier to spread out and handle. Others spit on the shoe as they squat to polish, a technique meant to add extra shine.

The oldest group, from sixteen to twenty, are known as Cowboys. Strutting about in pastel shirts, tilted cotton hats, and tight slacks, they are often army deserters or former shoeshine boys whose petty crimes have escalated into more violent ones. Traveling in gangs of three or four, they steal, mug, and even murder as the occasion arises. Like weeds that have been allowed to grow wild, they now choke the roots of the society that spawned them. They represent the ultimate degradation awaiting the street child in any country that cannot care for its young.

TUNG

Tung looks younger than his nine years. Because he has an attractive, waiflike quality, he finds he can beg instead of work to get money. A year ago he sold chewing gum in downtown Saigon for an older woman, but he fought a lot with the other children and was eventually fired. He doesn't want to shine shoes until he has to.

At night Tung sleeps in a ragtag pile of other children on the steps of one of Saigon's largest movie theaters.

"I like to live on the streets," he says cheerfully in pidgin English, as he puffs on a cigarette an American soldier has given him. "Mom no can tell me what to do."

Most of the street children who hang out with him do not talk about their backgrounds, but Tung readily admits to having run away from his home on the outskirts of Saigon two years ago. As he explains it, his father was in the army and his mother screamed too much. So he left.

Tung is the youngest of six children. Two of his brothers are in the army and two sisters sell cigarettes on the streets of Tay Ninh, a provincial city thirty miles from Saigon. He admits he misses his parents, even dreams about them at night on the steps of the theater, but he repeats, "It was no fun at home."

As he speaks, one can picture the exhausted mother anxiously dividing the inadequate portions of rice, desperately trying to figure out ways to exist until her husband returns. One can see Tung sitting there, dreaming of a better life in the freedom of the city streets rather than sharing the meager gruel at home and taking orders. With no male authority to stop him, Tung already was doing pretty much as he pleased. And so he set out to test his dream.

Tung has looked for his new life along with the other street children in the heart of Saigon near the bars where American soldiers come to drink and find the gentle comforts of home—a girl for the night. A GI becomes an older brother to some of the lonely boys. He can also become the father the child has never known. "Hey man," a dirty-faced youngster calls out to some soldier whose waist he hardly reaches, "You want my sister? She number one! She make you feel number one too!"

But Tung's dreams are not uninterrupted. From time to time when the children have collected together like too many pigeons in a park, the police swoop down and carry them off to jail. The penalty for vagrancy is four to six weeks.

"Vietnamese police number ten," says Tung, who has been harassed by them more times than he can count. If he is caught sleeping in front of a public building or makes trouble for a merchant by camping near a private store, off he goes in the green and white police jeep.

Tung is more careful now. At night one part of him is always alert. A part of Tung never sleeps.

When asked what he wants to be when he grows up, Tung looks puzzled, as if taken by surprise. Until now he has been living only in the present, getting through each day as if it existed in a vacuum by itself, as if there were no future. And he is not alone in this. Because of the hunger, pain, and experience with death, Vietnamese children have learned early to expect little from life. It is enough for them to meet the difficult demands of the present. The future will have to take care of itself.

Unlike American children who seek happiness in each waking moment, many Vietnamese children seem to live in a limbo between the hope of better days and the despair of their broken lives. Happiness and sadness are linked. "In happiness there is always sadness, and in sadness, one feels some happiness," a Vietnamese will often say. "Things won't get much better, but neither will they get much worse."

And yet children like Tung often find that each day can get worse.

"What do I want to be when I grow up?" He repeats the question. And then he suddenly knows.

"A soldier. I want to be a soldier and carry a gun."

"Why?"

"When I die, I will be buried. And I never look for a place to sleep at night again."

Tung smiles and then laughs openly. The other "Dust of Life" children laugh too. Soon the air is filled with the strange, hollow laughter of children who are no longer young.

LY

> A bankrupt society will alienate its most promising youth. Individuals with relatively high intuitive personal standards find it impossible to operate in an atmosphere of extreme conflict, deception, and congestion. And so it is with many of the street boys of Vietnam.
>
> DICK HUGHES, DIARY

Fourteen-year-old Nguyen Van Ly lives with twenty other shoe-shine boys in a small shelter in Saigon they call home. It is one of several such houses set up a few years ago by Donald Ronk, a former International Volunteer Services member. Ronk moved on to Laos, but Dick Hughes, who came to Vietnam as a free-lance journalist, stepped in and has remained to run the hostels. Even the street boys who have not accepted his hospitality know that this twenty-eight-year-old American is a foreigner they can trust.

Most Americans are not in Vietnam by choice, but because of the war. Few have a knowledge of the language, or the time or even the curiosity to look beyond their own activities. Few really see into the faces of the people, especially those of the street children.

Dick Hughes took the time and became imprisoned by what he

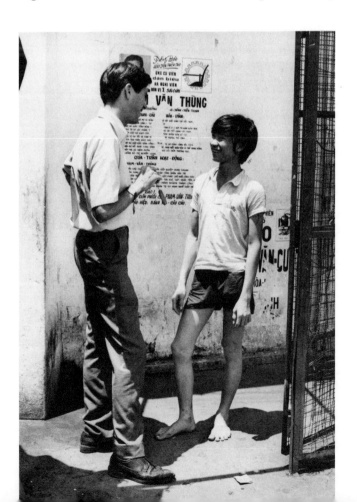

saw. In his eyes the boys were acutely sensitive, imaginative, and receptive children. He decided to create a place where they could live and learn to care about themselves again.

Ly heard about the shoeshine center from some of the street children he hung around with after running away from home three years before. He says he left because his mother had died and his father remarried a woman he couldn't get along with. When he approached Hughes, he had already lost a sense of direction for his life. His aimless wandering had taken its toll.

The Vietnamese staff at the shelter knew that they had to motivate Ly to help him find a goal.

Ly could not believe the world he had stepped into. For the first time he was being accepted for what he was. He and the other boys had a place to sleep, to shower, to store their clothes and wooden shoeshine kits. They had a safe area for their money and access to some medicines. They could go to the Saigon University dental school clinic to have their teeth fixed, and to the Seventh-Day Adventist Hospital for free medical help. They received two meals a day, blankets, soap, towels, toothbrushes, and clothes.

Ly saw too that the demands and regimentation were kept at a minimum. He had the freedom to come and go as he chose.

At first Ly decided he wanted to be a bricklayer like his father, but he soon gave that idea up. Then he wanted to be a mechanic. But that idea was quickly forgotten.

Finally Hughes, who has trained as an actor, introduced Ly to a local musical comedy group, a *cai luong* troupe, which does traditional South Vietnamese theater. The troupe was the poorest of five in Saigon, and they were glad to have him help clear the stage, set lights, and dress the actors. Ly even played the small part of a soldier once and was promoted to play a mandarin in the next production.

After a few months, however, the newness faded and Ly decided to leave the group. He wanted to learn to play the drums, but Hughes did not encourage this. He was afraid of the negative influence of hip young musicians.

And so Ly is now living at the house quietly once again, between jobs, waiting.

"He is an open and gentle boy," Hughes says. "Violence startles him. A strange quality for a street boy, but he hasn't given up believing that the intentions of others are good. I think that once given an opportunity for schooling, he will do rather well."

This period of idleness seems not to bother Ly either. He jokingly refers to the blue dot he has scratched on his forehead just above his nose as the mark of the Bui Doi.

Using the same sharp pen, he has also tattooed a heart on his arm with the initials DTV inside. In Vietnamese they mean "Golden Shining Heart." On his leg he has written the Vietnamese proverb, "Although blood flows back to the heart, no one can stop the eagle from flying." What does it mean? He says it is the story of his life. Blood must return to the heart just as children must return to their parents. But no one can stop the eagle, himself, from flying.

What he is really saying is that he sees himself as society sees him—a powerful, uncontrollable boy—but that he must be this way to be free like the eagle.

These tattoos, often profound in their meaning, are popular with all street boys. Ly's friend has written "A Lonely Man" in English on his arm. It is as if these tattoos are the boys' secret messages to the world, unique gestures of self-identification and, perhaps, cries for help.

Meanwhile, Ly eats at the center and has few expenses. He says he is living on the money earned with the theater group. He often sleeps until noon. At night he stays up late talking, watching TV, or walking the streets.

As for the future, Ly just shrugs. He says he will have to become a soldier someday, and that he will probably run away from the army.

Recently Hughes turned the complete workings of the five shelters over to his Vietnamese staff. He realizes the people of Vietnam must run their own hostels, just as they must run their own country. With increasingly less financial support coming from American donors, the centers will need more Vietnamese assistance if they are to survive. They may not.

There are some Vietnamese who say that the shelters have outlived their purpose, that many of the boys would return home if the hostels did not exist. Hughes does not agree.

"The boys would stay on the streets rather than go back to a dismembered family that is both desperate and in despair," he says. "And whether or not the countryside is secure is irrelevant. The kids don't believe it, so they're not going back out yet."

Hughes sees the Bui Doi's future in Saigon as bleak. With the American pullout of troops and no more shoes to shine, they will revert to theft. And new children will hit the streets when their parents lose the jobs they had at the American bases and can't find work.

"If they can have meals and board at the hostels, it will keep them from drugs and crime," Hughes says. "When they're out alone, living in the streets, anything goes. The war has made them frightful realists, all-or-nothing gamblers."

Hughes is leaving the future open. "Like the kids, I find it is the only way to fly." But he knows that even when he returns to a career in theater in his own country, he will not be free of these boys who are so much a part of him.

In his diary he has written, "They will be with me on the windy beach walk. They will be with me in a makeup room or on a stage. And in the early morning hours. Will I keep the joy they have taught me? . . ."

PRISONERS

A visit to Te Ban prison today. Futility. Absolute futility.

DICK HUGHES

The scenario was simple enough. As the war continued to drag on, more and more of the street boys found drugs an irresistible solution to their problems. They started out casually as middlemen between the procurers and the addicts. Then gradually they became the addicts themselves. It made them feel alive in a land where there was so little opportunity. With their quick wits and nimble feet they could get whatever the soldiers craved: marijuana; amphetamine stimulants to be injected or taken in pills; and cigarettes mixed with marijuana and heroin.

When the crackdown on drugs in the American military came, it was the street boys who were caught. The "mama-sans" who organize much of the activity in the back alleys could pay off. But the children were helpless and ended up in prison with serious charges of drug running and addiction.

In America we know that prisons are often better at breeding hardened criminals than reformed citizens. In Vietnam this is also true. The boys are not separated by age, but are thrown in with thieves and murderers, as well as political prisoners.

Visit the provincial prison just outside of Nha Trang. It holds eight hundred and forty prisoners, one tenth of whom are young drug offenders.

One of them, Phan Bach, is sixteen. He sleeps at night with fifty other prisoners of all ages in a tall cement-block cell connected to the outside by a small barred window.

Phan Bach was stopped by police while carrying heroin—smack —which he was accustomed to injecting five times a day while procuring for American soldiers. He was thrown into prison and given no assistance during his harrowing withdrawal period.

"I cried with agony," he says, "beat my head against the wall, and begged the other prisoners to knock me unconscious. My stomach, oh, my stomach. The pain was too much. I closed my

eyes and wanted to sleep, but each time I could only see the needle pushing smack into my vein.

"I still cannot sleep," he continues. "Only cigarettes help to stop the pain."

He sits on a prison bench, his face strained, his hands clasped around his thin knees. At times he speaks Vietnamese, at times the slangy pidgin English he picked up from the American soldiers and bar girls.

"No one says when the pain will end," he goes on. "No one tells me how long I stay here."

In yet another cell is Tran Tan, age fifteen. He was working in a bar frequented by American soldiers, when friends asked him to sniff some white powder they were peddling. It made him feel strong and happy. Within a month he was injecting heroin into his arm twice a day.

Discussing his habit, Tan says, "Many of my friends smoke the white powder. I used to know boys in Saigon who sold it to Americans. I was afraid I would not be able to buy it when I moved to Nha Trang. But now I know there is no problem. If you want to buy it anywhere, it's there. All you need is money."

Nguyen Thanh, at thirteen, is the youngest prisoner in his cell block.

Thanh started off carrying small vials of heroin from the tobacco store near the market to downtown Nha Trang. By the time he was picked up by the Vietnamese police, he had grown to enjoy the powder—and was feeding a habit of two vials a day.

The boys will have to wait six to eight months before they come to trial. In a country at war, the courts are filled with more important offenders than street boys.

According to the prison warden, they will not be released until they are eighteen. In Thanh's case, that will be five years.

And so with thousands of other young prisoners they wait. For just a short while they had found in drugs what American GI's were trying to find—a momentary release from the misery around them, an illusion of a happier world. Now they are back in the reality of Vietnam.

A Saigon Hippie

"I Feel Like I'm Fixin' To Die" Rag

Come on all of you big strong men
Uncle Sam needs your help again
He's got himself in a terrible jam
Way down yonder in Vietnam
So put down your books and pick up a gun
We're gonna have a whole lot of fun.

And it's 1, 2, 3, what are we fighting for?
Don't ask me I don't give a damn
Next stop is Vietnam
And it's 5, 6, 7, open up the Pearly Gates
Well there ain't no time to wonder why
Whoopee we're all gonna die.

Well come on Generals let's move fast
Your big chance has come at last
Gotta go out and get those Reds
The only good Commie is the one that's dead
And you know the peace can only be won
When we've blown them all to kingdom come.

Well come on mothers throughout the land
Pack your boys off to Vietnam
Come on fathers don't hesitate
Send your son before it's too late
Be the first one on your block
To have your boy come home in a box.

COUNTRY JOE MCDONALD

Love Song

I had a lover who died at the battle of Pleime,
I had a lover who died at Battle Zone "D",
Who died at Dong Xoai,
Who died at Hanoi,
He died far away on the distant frontier.

I had a lover who died in the battle of Chu Prong,
I had a lover whose body drifted along a river,
Who died in the dark forest,
Whose charred body lies cold and abandoned.

I want to love you, love Viet Nam,
The day when the wind is strong
I whisper your name, the name of Viet Nam,
We are so close, the same voice and yellow race.
I want to love you, Viet Nam.

I had a lover who died at Ashau,
I had a lover whose twisted body lies in a valley,
Who died under a bridge, naked and voiceless.
I had a lover who died at the Battle of Ba Gia,
I had a lover who died last night,
He passed away as in a dream.

TRINH CONG SON

THE WEALTH THAT THE PROFITS OF WAR HAVE BROUGHT TO MANY Saigon families has had a double edge. It has enabled them to live in luxury in a time of misery. But it has distorted the values of their children, many of whom seem to have become grotesque caricatures of the American youth culture. Familes that thought they could have their imported Mercedes Benz, Johnnie Walker whisky, deep freezes, washing machines, and air conditioning, while retaining the traditional values of their ancestors, are aghast to find their young are pursuing materialism and sex as a way of life.

Many of the teenagers from upper-class families own Hondas and ride the streets of Saigon in tight, stylish shirts and pocketless pants that cling to their legs. While four years ago only bar girls wore Western dress, today's teenage girls wear miniskirts, having given up their long white flowing *ao dais,* just as they have given up the chastity with which these garments are associated.

Sixteen-year-old Vo Dinh Hien spends most of his waking hours stoned, listening to Western hard rock music with friends in the Bo Da ice cream parlor located on Tu Do Street—a center for American-style bars and nightclubs. He likes to pass the time watching Americans drink beer and pick up girls.

"I don't think of tomorrow," says Hien, scooping out multi-flavored ice cream served in a coconut shell. "Whatever I want to do, I do. I sleep where I want and with whomever I like. I am free." As Hien spoke, his sixteen-year-old girl friend, dressed in a flowered miniskirt, sat snuggled beside him. She punctuated his

57

statements with embarrassed giggles.

Hien estimates that more than half the high-school girls in Saigon share his values. "Even the girls who still wear ao dais secretly like me," he says, running his hands through his black hair, which falls below his shoulders.

"I started growing my hair long a year and a half ago," he explains. "The police hate long hair. Sometimes they even stop us on the streets and cut it off with their bayonets."

It seems Hien's parents also disapproved of his long hair, nor could they tolerate his listening to rock music instead of studying. He was finding it increasingly difficult to explain his ways to them, for though they had lived in Saigon for ten years, they had grown up in a village not far from the capital and still held its traditional values. When the tensions became too great, he left home, school, and family ties for a life with other hippie friends who were already dropouts or were contemplating the possibility.

Compared to the others in his crowd, Hien's parents are not wealthy. He owns only three shirts and three pairs of pants, which he keeps in the homes of whatever friends he is hanging out with at the moment.

"Fun depends on one important factor—money," he declares. "You must have money in Vietnam to do what you like. With a thousand dollars I could even buy my way out of the army.

"Of course, money cannot make one happy," he concedes, "but it can put one in a position to be happy. Nothing is more important in my life than money." He emphasizes this by clenching his fist with his thumb pointing upwards, a gesture meaning "number one" in the jargon of the young.

"Money is number one! It buys smack and girls. And that's what life is all about!"

How did he get into drugs?

"About six months ago I was with some friends who smoked dope," he replies. "I tried it. It helped me hear each musical note. So I began smoking every day."

Three months later, also under the influence of friends, he began smoking heroin because the kick was stronger.

Of course, his habit takes money. Hien concedes he has to work occasionally. He pimps or hires himself out do do any task asked of him. Last week, he says, he beat up a student because someone paid him twenty dollars.

"I work and I play. When the money's gone, I get some more," he adds, laughing, and exhales the smoke of a Salem cigarette.

The talk at the Bo Da ice cream parlor never drifts far from the subject of rock music. Everyone listens daily to the American Armed Forces Network, which plays rock much of the time. Saigon stations play only Vietnamese music, which the boys find boring.

"Once you've heard American and English rock, Vietnamese music is no longer worth listening to," Hien explains.

Hien and his friends also prefer foreign movies to the popular Vietnamese plays, which take the form of love dramas and slapstick comedies. "The best movie to come to Vietnam in the last year was *Woodstock*," he says. "We just got high, walked in, and sat down."

Hien says he has no political sense. He has given no thought to what life might be like if the Communists were to achieve success in the South.

But he adds quickly, "I'm for peace. All hippies are for peace. The war is not our war, so let someone else worry about it. I just want to enjoy my life."

Still he knows he'll have to go into the Army in two years when he turns eighteen. "I want to have no regrets when I go in," he confides. "So I do exactly what I like now. It's not that I hate the army. But I don't want to be a soldier. I'd rather be free."

Will he always seek the hippie life style?

"I don't know," he admits after pausing for a few moments. And then, ignoring the giggles of his girl friend, he declares, "When I do marry, it will be to a good girl who has not played around with other boys.

"Anyway, who can say what life will be like in five or ten years," Hien concludes as he and his friends walk out of the ice cream parlor on their way to the Hondas, which will carry them off to the next coffee shop. Raising two fingers for peace and crossing palms —the hippie handshake—they depart.

Although Hien and his friends have no desire to ride out into the countryside—"peasants are good people, but backward"—there is little doubt they would gladly ride ten thousand miles over the seas to that fabled land, the Mecca of hippies, which they spend so many hours dreaming about.

An Amerasian Boy

"Sacrifice me alone and save our home: one flower will fall, but green will stay the tree."

NGUYEN DU
The Tale of Kim Van Kieu

"Nobody could really understand the *Kim Van Kieu* but the Vietnamese. Perhaps a Jew can understand Vietnamese history, an Irishman the Vietnamese romantic mind, the Russian the Vietnamese pessimism, and the Italian the Vietnamese sense of optimism and drama. No one, no American, can be a mixture of all these."

TRAN VAN DINH
"Why Every American Should Read Kim Van Kieu"

BLACK BOY IS TOO YOUNG TO REMEMBER WHEN HIS AMERICAN
father rotated back to the United States, leaving him and his
mother with promises of letters and money. Three years have
passed since then, and his father, like so many other servicemen,
has disappeared into the vast country across the sea.

Besides broken promises, American soldiers and civilians have
left tens of thousands of mixed-blood children like Black Boy behind. For the Western world, these men are merely modern Lieu-
tenant Pinkertons saying their eternal farewells to Madame Butter-
fly. For the Vietnamese, they are another manifestation of the
hordes of foreigners who have raped Vietnam over the centuries.
And women like Black Boy's mother are modern incarnations
of the beautiful, ill-fated Kieu, heroine of Vietnam's most famous
epic poem, *The Tale of Kim Van Kieu.*

Kieu, who has more counterparts in Asian than Western litera-
ture, was a maiden with filial piety and "pale fate." When her
father and brother were unjustly threatened with debtor's prison,
she gave up all hope of marriage to her fiancé and sold herself into
prostitution. For the next fifteen years of "winds and rain," she
suffered so many misfortunes and indignities that a less hardy soul
would have been destroyed. But in the end she found spiritual
peace and was reunited with her family and lost love. Many Vietnamese consider her tale an inspiration in enduring the hardships
of the present war.

Black Boy's mother, thirty-seven-year-old Tuyet, led a quiet life

63

in a rural village much as Kieu had in her youth. But here the analogy ends and the modern tale takes on the twist of modern history.

Tuyet's husband, a Vietnamese, left her with an infant girl when he was drafted into the South Vietnamese army in 1965. He has not been heard from since. Her destitute family, like so many in the countryside, soon realized that their best chance of survival lay in sending their daughter to work near Americans who controlled the wealth.

Drifting into Nha Trang to find some employment, Tuyet stumbled upon the Jackie Bar. The owner told her she could sell drinks to the servicemen during hours, with nothing more being asked of her. But Tuyet soon found that she could earn much more money after the bar closed—indeed, more money than most small businessmen. It was then that she met Black Boy's father, Freddie.

Tuyet still refers to Freddie as her "husband." She recalls that they ate well and had enough to pay the rent for their three-room cement house. But shortly after Black Boy was born, Freddie, a sergeant in the army, had completed his year of duty and was sent home.

"He say he come back. I believe him," Tuyet says in halting English. "I know what other men like, but not Freddie. He good. I think he come back Vietnam."

Now Tuyet has another baby by a soldier who also served his year in Vietnam and left. She no longer thinks fondly of Freddie.

"Now I know he number ten," she says, shaking her head. This is the lowest designation one can give. "I throw away his picture. I have no husband for my boys. No money for food. We very poor. Very sad."

Tuyet cannot understand how Freddie could abandon his boy. She cannot believe he does not care enough about his child to send money for support, even if he has another family back home.

In the epic novel, Kieu herself drew strength at the grave of a famous songstress who in her life was a wife to everyone and in death a ghost without a husband. Today, women like Tuyet draw strength from the memory of Kieu's ordeals as they experience temporary arrangements with American servicemen who serve one year of duty and move on. They see themselves as selling their bodies but not their souls in order to help their families.

The modern tale of Kieu would also have to include the "pale fate" of children like Black Boy, who are the offspring of war's distorted passion. Nha Trang, where he was born, is one of the

most beautiful seashore towns in South Vietnam. But the sprawl of back alleys where he is growing up is a Vietnamese slum not unlike those of his father's homeland. When he goes outside to play, he cautiously stays on the sidelines and watches. He is either ignored or taunted by the other children. "My den! my den!" (black American), they call out—which is how he got his name. On some days he may hear a neighboring woman tease his mother: "Is that your child?"

Of course, mixed-blood children are not a new phenomenon in Vietnam, which was under French rule for three quarters of a century. But the magnitude of the situation is altogether new. Nearly ten times as many Americans were there between 1965 and 1970 as Frenchmen throughout the entire colonial period.

As yet there is no name for American-fathered children, like the French-fathered *métis* or the European-fathered Eurasian or the Anglo-Indian in India. However, they are increasingly being referred to as Amerasians.

The United States government has taken no responsibility for Amerasians like Black Boy, as the French did for the métis. (They were given French citizenship upon request and an allotment for education in Vietnam or France.) The Department of Defense issued a paper in 1970 stating that "the care and welfare of these unfortunate children" was not an appropriate mission for it to assume.

The Saigon government officially denies the problem of racially mixed children, as if it does not exist.

At the present time American welfare agencies are trying to push a modest bill through Congress that would facilitate intercountry adoption and social welfare programs for *all* Vietnamese children. But there are no provisions in it for special support for Amerasians, which they believe would set these children apart from their Vietnamese siblings and segregate them even more within society. As yet the American government is under no pressure to recognize the children its troops are fathering overseas.

Amerasians like Black Boy continue to grow up in poor, broken homes with no outside help. As American troops pull out, their mothers are losing the employment they had in the false economy of the bars and brothels around United States bases. They have even fewer means of taking care of their fatherless children.

Yet Black Boy is more fortunate than the large number of Amerasians in orphanages, who were abandoned at birth because of the shame they represented to their mothers. Fifty per cent of those children are black.

Black Boy is too young to understand all this as he stands wistfully watching the neighborhood children play. He is still too innocent to know he is being rejected for the darkness of his skin as well as the mixture of his blood. For the Vietnamese have always had disdain for the more primitive dark-skinned mountain tribesmen (the Montagnards), and class prejudice against peasants, whose faces have been darkened by their labor in the fields. White Amerasians will fare somewhat better than Black Boy, although they too will find difficulty in employment and marriage.

Were Black Boy older, he would probably be on the streets, shining American shoes or hanging around his mother's bar, selling cigarettes or drugs. Now all he can do is stand around the alley, occasionally scratching at the white ointment his mother has rubbed into his scalp to help the skin disease that does not disappear. With his meager diet of occasional pig's skin, dried fish, cut-up leaves, and rice, he already shows symptoms of the protein and vitamin deficiency so common among Vietnamese children— fragile bones and various skin ailments. Since he probably will get little if any education, he will most likely end up as a cycle driver, a soldier, or a common laborer.

Looking into Black Boy's forlorn face, one has a sense one has seen it before—in Korea, in Japan, in Thailand—in every Asian country where the American military has sent its forces. The skin lighter or darker, the features slightly rearranged, each face bears the confusion of the child's identity, the stigma of his birth, and the hopelessness of his future.

Rejected by both the East and the West, from what heritage can mixed-blood children like Black Boy draw their strength? Perhaps they, like their mothers, can find solace in the final verses of *The Tale of Kieu:*

All things are fixed in heaven, first and last.
Heaven assigns each creature to a place.
If we are marked for grief, we'll come to grief.
We'll win high state when high state is our lot.

Each one of us has a Karma to live:
let's stop decrying Heaven's quirks and whims.
Deep inside us there lies the root of good:
the heart means more than all talents on earth.

The War Wounded

War seems to be quite merciless nowadays. We read in our history books that bodies used to be piled up like mountains and blood flowed like rivers. But even that couldn't match the horror of this war.

NGOC KY
"A Visit To My Village"
Between Two Fires

We talk about new hospitals and more staff, but nothing will be right for these people until the war is over. The war must stop. We must argue hard to justify these wounds. The real answer to the civilian war-wounded is to stop shooting at them.

NEW ZEALAND DOCTOR
Qui Nhon Provincial Hospital

NO ONE WILL EVER KNOW THE EXACT NUMBER OF CHILDREN killed and wounded in this war. Only those who live to make it to the hospitals are ever counted. They are brought by parents or relatives in sampans or carts; some are picked up by American helicopters. But no one knows how many are killed instantly, die in transit, are too weak to be moved, or are in Viet Cong-controlled areas to which there is no access.

Walking through the hot, overcrowded hospital wards in Vietnam, one can see children lying two to a bed or on stretchers on the floor. There are children burned like paper dolls by napalm, paralyzed children as still as the air. Children who have lost arms and legs. Children receiving free limbs from USAID the way our children receive lollipops. A gift from the generous Americans. A souvenir of war.

Some of these children were riding water buffalo when the American planes came overhead. Some were in their beds asleep with their younger brothers and sisters when the exploding shells ripped through their dreams. Some were caught in the crossfire of soldiers fighting to regain a village. Some stepped on mines. Some simply do not know what happened.

Some, like Vo Tanh, know but can no longer communicate their experience. For Vo Tanh is deaf, dumb, blind and missing one hand as a result of the war. He was found by American soldiers lying on a deserted road north of Saigon, his head and arms riddled by shell fragments. It is believed he was playing with an explosive

71

that went off in his face.

The Americans took Vo Tanh to their army base, which transferred him quickly to a Vietnamese hospital. After emergency treatment—there was no time for more thorough care with wounded soldiers needing help—he was sent to a nearby home for the elderly run by old men who also took in a few children in desperate need of shelter.

The aged men did not know what to do with this blind boy who had lost his power of speech and went into tantrums to make his wishes known. In desperation they tied him by his only wrist to a bedpost to keep him from running away or bothering the others.

After several months a social worker found Vo Tanh in the home. Alarmed by his bleeding, rope-burned wrist, his shrapnel-filled eyes and infected ears, she took him to the provincial hospital. It was there that a representative for the Committee of Responsibility came upon him.

COR, as this American-funded group of doctors and laymen is known, had been negotiating for almost a year with the reluctant Vietnamese government to allow badly wounded children to be flown to the United States for treatment. Both Saigon and Washington resisted its efforts, maintaining that the children should be treated in their homeland rather than be uprooted. But considering the inadequate facilities in Vietnam, the real reason seemed to be the fear that these mutilated youngsters might stimulate antiwar sentiment in America. Finally a compromise was reached. COR was permitted to fly out about seventy-six wounded children to hospitals in various parts of the States. Vo Tanh was in one of the first groups.

Since his identity was unknown, COR changed the Vietnamese word for "nameless," Vo Ten, to Vo Tanh.

The boy was sent first to the Massachusetts Eye and Ear Infirmary in Boston, where one eye was removed and operations were performed on his ears, to stop the infections that endangered his life. Metal fragments were removed from his face. A spring brace was designed for his shoe to help support a drop foot not correctable by operation.

From the hospital Vo Tanh was taken to the Perkins School for the Blind. There he was introduced to Christopher Huggins, who became his tutor and personal companion, as well as his link to the outside world during the initial stages of his rehabilitation. His relationship to Huggins was not unlike Helen Keller's with Annie Sullivan during the years she struggled out of her dark and silent world. The difference was that Vo Tanh was aware of what language meant, but seemed unprepared to use it.

During those early months at Perkins, Vo Tanh behaved like a wild animal, throwing his tantrums and showing no desire to feed or toilet himself. He screamed for hours in high-pitched sounds—desperate and frantic pleas to the darkened world to leave him alone.

The twenty-four-year-old Huggins tried to stop Vo Tanh's tantrums by embracing the boy, then letting him be. It became a matter of containing him gradually and building his trust.

The staff at Perkins was confused when Vietnamese interpreters brought in to communicate with their patient could not get through to him. With the help of a powerful hearing aid, he could obviously hear some of their sounds, but showed no recognition of the language that had once been his. The trauma of his experience seemed to have caused a kind of amnesia.

Huggins was encouraged by the examination of a doctor who said that the boy suffered no visible brain damage from the accident, that he might talk again if he could overcome his "psychological defenses."

Gradually Huggins was able to gain Vo Tanh's trust. He was particularly encouraged when the boy started to keep time with his fingers to the low, sonorous tones of the Perkins bells. Before long he could count up to twenty-nine in English. He could approximate sounds like *man, woman, car, airplane, foot, how, hello, good-by, yes,* and *no.* He could say about five proper names, among them Ronnie, the name of another blind boy at the school of whom he was fond, and of course that of his best friend, Mr. Huggins. He even began learning to type in Braille. He was revealing himself as a remarkably perceptive and intelligent human being.

"One could tell, even from the darting eye that couldn't see, that this boy had been bright," says Huggins. "The way he fearlessly walked around the grounds alone or helped the other, more hesitant children, like Ronnie, to find their way. I had the feeling that Vo Tanh had been an aggressive, quick, agile, clever, independent leader of his friends."

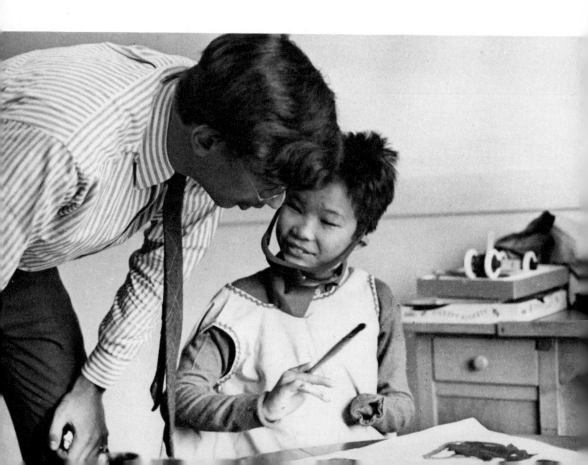

Part of COR's agreement with the Vietnamese government was that the children would all be returned to their own country. And so last year Vo Tanh was flown back to Saigon. Huggins traveled with him and stayed for two months at the COR house in Saigon while his pupil learned to transfer his needs to Co Nhan, a twenty-seven-year-old Vietnamese speech therapist.

"Although he had been fearful at the prospect of returning to Vietnam, he soon seemed happy to be back," Huggins recalls. "The return to familiar surroundings, tastes, and smells stimulated many memories. When eating papaya for the first time, his face brightened up. He lifted his head, spreading his fingers to indicate 'tree,' and smiled to show that he knew where the fruit came from."

Such gestures are an important form of communication for Vo Tanh now, a way he can even initiate a conversation. He makes them with the enthusiasm we might have in a game of charades, revealing the sense of humor he must have had once as a village child.

"There is no question that he was from a village," says Huggins. "In his gestures one sees clearly the gaiety of a country boy, the impetuous youth in nature, fishing in the streams, hunting with slingshots, climbing trees for fruit.

"And yet, he seems to have many conflicting stories when I ask him about his past life," Huggins adds. "Once he indicated he ran away from home, and another time that his mother ordered him to leave. In one story he was even a soldier carrying a gun. I cannot separate the truth from what may be just the fantasies of youth."

But every now and then Vo Tanh has the need to repeat what seems to be his one most consistent story—the time he found the explosive in a tree. He acts out that fateful moment with vivid arm and body gestures. There he is once again, spotting something in

the branches. He takes a long object, perhaps a bamboo pole that he once used to guide his water buffalo. He hits it against the tree to get the object down. Now he is holding it, this possible plaything that seems a gift from the heavens meant just for him. Now it explodes in his face.

No matter how many times Vo Tanh relives his story in his gestures or his nightmares, there must remain the mystery that no one can answer for him. Where did they all go in that one moment—his village, his family, his friends? The boy he used to be?

Until someone claims him, Vo Tanh, who is now about sixteen, has just been entered in a school for the blind run by a Catholic Brother. He is learning to make brooms while he indulges in what is his greatest pleasure, smoking cigarettes. There, puffing away in darkness and almost total silence, whatever else he may be, Vo Tanh is a child of Vietnam.

MI

I could hear the planes still overhead, and the flares still dropping. I looked and it was a bizarre sight—a small silhouette of a boy, running around the paddy field, chasing after the sound of the C-123 above him, running as if he were flying a kite because his arms were raised and he seemed to be having fun. And then the tracers from the machine gun reached out for him like a distorted broken finger, and the kid danced away and fell to the ground. The drone of the plane continued and the new flare came down, and the little boy appeared again like a jumping jack, and he was chasing after the new sound of the plane as if he were caught up in an insane game of trying to leap up into the air after it. And this time the tracers of the machine gun reached him, and the boy fell, not as if he had chosen to fall in his wild hide-and-seek out there in the paddy field. The machine-gun bullets had killed him. I knew it. The machine gunner knew it, and the two Marines knew it. . . . We went out to where the body was and it was a little boy; he looked like eight, but he was probably twelve. The diet is poor in Vietnam and the bodies are smaller. He was lying down in the wet paddy field, and the machine-gun bullets had practically chopped him in half. In his hand were the parachutes from the flares he had been collecting.

DEAN BRELIS
The Face of South Vietnam

The hospital wards are filled with the broken bodies of the young who were betrayed in one way or another by the carnival mask of war. Nothing is more deceptive than the beauty of American flares, which drop in parachutes from the planes at night to light up enemy positions. They drift through the heavens like some great fireworks display, casting eerie shadows onto the walls of peasant huts where the children huddle together in fascination and fear.

Twelve-year-old Mi in the Children's Convalescent Center in Saigon knows about flares. A farmer's son from the village of Tay Ninh near the Cambodian border, he was familiar with the flight of birds and the movement of fish, but not the unnatural inventions of war.

Mi speaks through small lips encircled by globes of dripping, burned skin.

> How long have you been here, Mi?
> A long time.
> How long is a long time?
> I was wounded more than a year ago.
> Do you remember how it happened?
> I was coming home from school. Near my house was a friend who found an unignited flare. We looked at it to see what it could do. He hit it.

Mi stops talking for a while. Then haltingly he recalls that his friend was burned only below his knees. Already the nurses have explained that half of Mi's body was burned, that he has had two skin grafts and needs at least two more.

> Does it still hurt?
> No, the pain is not so much now. It itches a lot.

Mi looks down as he speaks. His voice has the softness of country children who have not been exposed to large urban centers. His burned fingers alternately play with a bandage on his right arm and then scratch at the burned body tissue swollen into pink and white lumps throughout his body.

> What do you remember about your home village?
> It was a place where people fight at night.
> Was anyone hurt in the fighting?

My oldest brother died three years ago. Death is
like my older brother was. Like those people who
fought.

Who fought, Mi?

The government soldiers and the Viet Cong—at
night. That's when people were afraid. I was afraid
too. The people die.

How often did they fight?

Every night they fight. I can't remember how many
times. So many times.

Why do they fight?

They fight because the Viet Cong comes.

Who are the Viet Cong?

The Viet Cong are people. I saw them when they
came to our house. I don't remember what they
said. It was a long time ago.

Mi's friends at the hospital do not understand the war any more
than he does. Dong, who is known as Older Brother by the children, lost his legs when the Lambretta he was riding in passed over
a mine. Now he rides a wheel chair through the wards. Six-year-old
Minh follows after him on metal crutches. Two plastic bags hang
from his side to catch urine and excrement. He lost a leg and his
genitals when he was hit by an American army truck on his way to
school outside of An Khe in central Vietnam.

Thirty per cent of the one hundred and twenty children in the
recuperation center run by the International Rescue Committee
are war-wounded. Other injuries were caused by fire from toppling
kerosene lamps, congenital defects, facial ulcers, and skin diseases

due to malnutrition. American doctors visit periodically, but most attention is given by the Vietnamese nurses.

There is an acute shortage of physicians for the civilian population, since most of them either serve in the military or have gone abroad to earn more money. Students from the Saigon Medical School are drafted upon graduation for the duration of the war. Only three hundred doctors are available to Saigon's population of three million. And a thousand others are scattered unevenly throughout this country of sixteen million.

Mi is one of the fortunate few who has been cared for by foreign-run organizations such as this one and the closely affiliated Children's Medical Relief International where he received his surgery.

He and the other maimed children do not like to speak about their sufferings. Unless prodded, they avoid thoughts that might embarrass them or bring back sad memories. They seem to have quietly accepted their fate just as they accept each other. No one child can point to another's affliction and laugh, as each lives with painfully visible scars and distortions. Their tragedies have made them more mature than other children their own age and given them a familial bond.

Mi's parents can visit him only once every two weeks, since their village is nearly one hundred miles away. The trip is long and arduous for them. His father is a farmer heavily in debt to the landlord whose fields he cultivates. His mother sells fruits at a local market near their home to help keep the large family of eight children on a subsistence level.

The nurses describe Mi as moody. At times he mingles freely among the others, picking "friendly fights," but often he just stays to himself. His favorite spot is in the branch of the tree in the hospital's enclosed courtyard. There he is, for a brief while, back with the buffaloes he used to ride or with his friends in the village school.

At night Mi plays marbles or watches television with Dong and Minh. The girls weave little baskets and hats out of plastic string. Patiently they all pass the time waiting for their bodies to mend— bodies which will never be what they were intended to be.

A Montagnard Girl

"Why do you like them so much? Montagnards are dirty."

A VIETNAMESE HIGH-SCHOOL
STUDENT

"The soldiers came to the borders of the village and forced us across the Niobrara to the other side, just as one would drive a herd of ponies. . . . We found the land there was bad and we were dying one after another, and we said, 'What man will take pity on us?' And our animals died. Oh, it was very hot. 'This land is truly sickly and we'll be apt to die here, and we hope the Great Father will take us back again.' That is what we said. There were one hundred of us died there."

WHITE EAGLE OF THE PONCAS
Bury My Heart at Wounded Knee
An Indian History of the American
West

NHER IS A MONTAGNARD GIRL. SHE IS ONE OF A DWINDLING number of primitive mountain people in the vast Central Highlands who are believed to be the original inhabitants of Vietnam. No group has suffered more from the war than these 800,000 Montagnards, whose name covers thirty main tribes, and comes from the French for "mountaineers."

Until recently their aboriginal culture was relatively untouched by modern civilization. The Vietnamese preferred to farm in the deltas and along the coast where wet rice grows best, and the French did not interfere with the mountaineers' customs.

It was not until shortly after Nher was born, fifteen or sixteen years ago—she is not sure which—that the full impact of the war began to invade the Montagnard sanctuaries. Both sides needed the tribesmen, who were at home in the rugged terrain of the jungles and mountains. To prevent the Viet Cong from using them as guides and a source for food supplies, the South Vietnamese government began forcibly moving seventy-five per cent of the Montagnard villagers to fortified areas. This dislocation has caused rampant outbreaks of diseases like T.B., cholera, and the plague, and death rates so high that some authorities fear the Montagnards may be headed for extinction.

For the past eighteen months Nher has been living with relatives in a small, isolated resettlement camp about twenty miles north of the city of Kontum and five miles from her former home. Her mother, father, and eight-year-old brother died from cholera when

it swept through their village three years ago. Her three older brothers were drafted into the Regional Forces, a paramilitary group organized by the South Vietnamese government. One of them died two months ago in an encounter with North Vietnamese soldiers.

"It was dark that night and we heard mortars landing nearby," Nher says. "We hid in our underground bunkers until it was quiet. Then we heard some more gunshots outside the village, and some shouting. But we were afraid to move. A little later they carried my brother into our house. He was bloody and I cried."

Tears fill her eyes as she adds, "I ask myself where my brother is. No one knows where he is."

Nher has only a nine-year-old sister left to share her lonely life with her. The girls often sit quietly together on a small mat spread on the dirt floor of their tin-roofed hut. Occasionally they just look into each other's eyes and smile gently.

They share memories of a time when they used to swim and fish and wash clothes in the fresh mountain stream that flowed near their village. In those days their tribe roamed the mountains, practicing a special kind of agriculture that involved burning part of the forest to clear land and farming it until the soil was depleted. Then they moved on to another area and repeated the same process until after a few years they returned to their original site. Their life, though circumscribed by the mountain range, had a sense of flow within it, not unlike that of the American Indians before they were confined to reservations.

Nher's relatives cannot farm adequately any more because their method needs space, and the territory around them is considered insecure. A Viet Cong-controlled hamlet is just one mile away. They must learn to work their small plots of land with the techniques of the lowland Vietnamese, who are as alien to them culturally and linguistically as the Americans who occasionally come through their villages. Each family grows some vegetables and manioc, but not enough for a healthy diet.

"Before, we were very rich," Nher says. "We lived in a big house. We had cows, water buffaloes, and chickens. Now we have nothing. We are very hungry. Life is sad here."

In the distance Nher can still see the mountain where she once lived. "That's where I was happy," she says, pointing toward it. "That's where I swam every afternoon."

For many animistic tribes like Nher's, the river, the source of fresh water and fish, is the mystical source of life. There is no mountain stream near Nher's resettlement camp. Water can be collected only when it rains. The tribespeople have asked the government to help them dig a well because they lack the proper tools, but they have not had a response.

Only half of the two thousand men, women, and children who

came with Nher to this camp remain. Disease has taken some; the armies of both sides have taken the others. Since fighting is the only way to earn money, many tribesmen volunteered to work as mercenaries with the American Green Berets, whom they preferred to the South Vietnamese, who have always treated them as inferiors. But their enlistment has brought even more North Vietnamese attacks against their people in retaliation and added even more to the Montagnard death toll.

In the past, the weaving of skirts and blankets was one of the aborigines' main occupations. Now Nher finds some comfort at the loom she brought with her from her village. She is considered to be one of the best weavers among the few women who still have time to pursue this pastime. It is a source of income as well as pride, for she sells her cloth to the merchants who come through occasionally gathering goods for the market in Kontum.

Nher has kept her favorite creation for herself. She wears it when requested by visitors to the camp or on holidays. The nights when the moon is full are the most festive times.

"That's when we stay up late talking," she says. "When it's bright the soldiers do not move around and there is little fighting."

On these occasions she smokes pipes and cigarettes, but unlike the other young girls she doesn't care for tobacco. Perhaps because of the mountain cold, the tribespeople have always smoked (as well as consumed large quantities of rice wine), and it is not uncommon to see small children puffing on pipes.

Nher takes time from weaving only to cook for her relatives, who give her and her sister food in return. Usually she uses her weaving money to buy extra provisions for her sister so that she has enough to eat.

"Sometimes I am a good cook," she says. "Sometimes not."

Because of inadequate diet, Nher, like the other villagers, gets ill

often. She believes her poor health is related to bad spirits in the mountains.

"The waters of the river had good spirits," she says. "Now the good spirits are far away."

Since medicine is a relatively new idea among Montagnards, Nher just takes to her bed when she feels feverish. She lies there waiting for the bad spirits to leave and the fever to drop.

Montagnards who have had some schooling and believe more in modern medicine than spirits, say their people are dying because they do not eat adequately and cannot keep themselves clean as in the past. And although they have a resistance to malaria (which the lowland Vietnamese do not), they cannot fight off cholera, which at present is rampant in the mountains.

Nher has never gone to school and probably never will. In the old days the children had little more to do than play when they weren't needed in the fields to scare away the crows. Some missionaries have recently set up a school for the very young in Nher's camp. But their assistance, even with their medicines and clothes, does not solve the greatest problem—lack of food.

Nher's relatives and friends, like the Montagnards throughout the highlands, are continuing to die at a frightening pace: there is now a seventy-five per cent mortality rate for children under thirteen. And the average life span for an adult has dwindled to about twenty-five years.

No foreigner can adequately feel the pain Nher carries within her. With each death in her village, she says her weaving and her younger sister become more essential to her life. Her own battle is to keep death from taking over her loom.

A Girl of the NLF

"No Vietnamese can forget that Ho Chi
Minh was the first Vietnamese leader to
declare the independence of Vietnam. He
declared it an independent state in September 1945 and a free state in March 1946.
When Ho Chi Minh went to war, he
seemed to be the heir to the nationalist
tradition of his people."

ELLEN HAMMER
The Struggle for Indochina

"I joined the ranks of the liberation army
in answer to the call of the front for liberation of the South. . . . Now my life is full of
hardship—not enough rice to eat nor
enough salt to give a taste to my tongue,
nor enough clothing to keep myself warm.
But in my heart I keep loyal to the Party
and to my people. I am proud and happy."

EXCERPTS FROM THE DIARY OF A
VIET CONG SOLDIER, DO LUC
The Viet-Nam Reader

"The body is in prison,
The mind escapes outside."

HO CHI MINH

FIFTEEN-YEAR-OLD NGUYEN THI LIEN IS A CHILD OF THE National Liberation Front. She grew up in what she calls a "liberated" area, a Viet Cong-controlled village in the Mekong Delta. Now she lives in what is known as an Open Arms Center, a camp for NLF members who want to "give up the struggle," "rally" to the other side, or defect—depending on one's semantics.

Two years ago Lien's father "gave up the struggle," as he puts it, and brought his family to this camp. Before then Lien had been raised on the values and doctrines of the Viet Cong: that her people must fight to defeat the U.S. aggressors and Vietnamese traitors; that the independence of her country was the essence of Nationalism.

Lien's father still refers to the Viet Cong as "liberators" when he speaks. After his fields were destroyed by bombs and he could no longer support his family, he decided to trust the leaflets which were being dropped by American psychological warfare planes. They promised his family would be given complete amnesty if they entered an "Open Arms" center.

Most of the other "ralliers" at Lien's camp in My Tho give as their reason for "coming over" the unbearable life they led under the Allied bombing and artillery attacks. Some of the guerrilla fighters there stated a strong desire to return to their families, a dispute with a platoon leader, or simply a desire to rest.

Now Lien's family lives in a state of limbo between the lost past

92

and the uncertain future. In the camp Lien keeps a small vegetable patch, growing lettuce and beans. She does not participate in the indoctrination lectures the adults must attend. For her the everyday chores must go on no matter what side she lives under.

She tells her own story:

> I have eight brothers and sisters, but I am the oldest. So I have a big responsibility in our family. I have to feed and care for all the children.

What do you remember most about life in your former village as you were growing up?

The musical skits that were held one night a month in the marketplace. There were dances and songs that told us stories about our country, about how we must struggle to stay independent. Some of them were funny and we laughed. It was fun then. I also remember my small garden. I grew flowers and vegetables for the family.

What work did your parents do?

They farmed. They grew rice and vegetables.

Did you have enough to eat?

We were very poor, but we ate just enough to fill our stomachs.

Did you go to school or stay at home and work?

In the liberation zone there were teachers and we all went to the People's school. The teachers loved the children. They wanted everyone in the village to be able to read and write and count. It was fun. We met during the day until the American airplanes began bombing. Then we met at night so they wouldn't see us. But we were so afraid of the bombs it was impossible to study any more.

Do you remember the first time you heard an airplane coming to your village?

Yes, I was twelve then. The airplanes came and began shooting near the market. The people were all very afraid. I ran into our house and dropped down underneath the bed. After that we built a shelter under our house. I had the responsibility of bringing my younger brothers and sisters into it every time I saw an airplane or helicopter, even if it was far away.

Did the different planes fight in different ways?

The B-52's (she uses their proper title) came very fast. We just heard the bombs, but we did not see the airplanes. At the first sound, we would grab everything and run for the shelter.

How many times each week did airplanes bomb?

Three times, sometimes four. Sometimes during the day, sometimes at night. The most dangerous hours were between midnight and four when it began to get light. There was much fighting then.

How many airplanes came at one time?

Sometimes ten or twelve. At night we were afraid and could not sleep.

Did any Northern soldiers come to your village?

No, only the guerrillas from the Delta.

Were you afraid of them?

I was not afraid of those who lived in the village. But I was afraid when they came from other villages because when they arrived the airplanes followed and the fighting began.

Did the soldiers in the Liberation Front give you food?

No, we gave food to them.

Do you know why the soldiers in the NLF are fighting?

They fight with the soldiers of the Republic of

Vietnam to liberate the people and the country.

Who are they liberating them from?

They are liberating them from the government of South Vietnam and the Americans who captured the country.

(At this point in the interview, which was watched by Lien's parents and a few trusted friends, word was passed to her to be careful not to say too much. They were fearful she would reveal something that would get the family into trouble.)

Do you remember seeing any Americans?

Not in the village. When we fled to the province, I saw some. They were like I heard they were. Very big with very long noses. I was afraid but I did not tell anyone.

(The Mekong Delta saw the fewest American combat soldiers of any region in Vietnam. The artillery and bombings, however, were principally carried out by Americans.)

I was also afraid of the soldiers of the Republic of Vietnam. They came into our houses and took our food. They stole our chickens, ducks, and pigs. They shot their guns to frighten us. Soon the villagers began to flee the soldiers and bombings.

How did you flee?

We got up in the morning at four. I cooked rice for the family which was all we had to eat. Then we took our things, and the women and children fled to another marketplace. I cried a lot then. I was tired and hungry and we were running from the fighting. The noise of bombings and artillery was very loud. And the people were wounded and dying.

Did you see anyone die?

My mother's younger brother. I saw the men carrying him home one day. His face was bloody. I knew he was dead. I cried and stayed in the house. Some of the houses were bombed. I could not understand why so many people wanted to kill the villagers.

(Lien's father broke in to explain it was about that time that the "struggle" became too great for him. He was overwhelmed with the difficulties of fighting for eight years to liberate his country. Life is easier for him now at the center, he said, for he does not have to "struggle" any more. He just waits for the day the war ends and he can return to his village with his family. Then he sat back and let Lien continue.)

Do you study now?

No, I cook and wash dishes and take care of my younger brothers and sisters. That is my responsibility.

Do you want to return to your village?

No, I do not want to go back there. Life was so difficult with the fighting and bombing.

Do you want to return in the future when the war ends?

I am afraid they will fight if we return.

I mean if there is peace?

I am afraid they will come again and shoot. And it will all be the same.

What do you want to do in the future when you leave here?

I want to sell food in the market.

(The interview was interrupted here by some officials at the center who came to "watch" what we were doing. Soon it became clear it was impossible to continue and get any further honest answers.)

The Children of My Lai

"When they died, they didn't know why
they were dying. And the people who were
doing the killing, they didn't know why
they were killing."

GI AT MY LAI
My Lai 4,
Seymour Hersh

"Humanity is mad! It must be mad to do
what it is doing. What a massacre! What
scenes of horror and carnage! I cannot find
words to translate my impressions. Hell
cannot be so terrible. Men are mad!"

FRENCH OFFICER, WORLD WAR I
The Price of Glory,
Alistair Horne

As we came to the conclusion of this book, we realized that there was still one story that had to be told. The story of the children who survived at My Lai.

But how does one tell about that massacre? Where does one begin?

These are the facts: On the morning of March 16, 1968, the American troops of Charlie Company landed by helicopter outside a small hamlet in Quang Ngai province known to them as My Lai 4. Their way had been paved for the past hour by heavily armed helicopters shooting artillery over the area. The soldiers of Charlie Company were under the impression that they were about to encounter a crack Viet Cong battalion. They found instead unarmed old men, women and children. When they left a few hours later, almost five hundred of the villagers were dead. Whole families had been slaughtered, together with their livestock. Even babies at their mothers' breasts had not been spared.

The Western world was stunned when the full details of the massacre were revealed a year and a half later in the court-martial of Lt. William L. Calley, Jr., the only one convicted for what happened at My Lai. Americans are still trying to comprehend the full significance of this atrocity. Some say that My Lai will go down in history as a symbol of what the United States has done to Vietnam. Others that is an example of how this war has brutalized American soldiers. And still others that it was a regrettable, but not unusual, consequence of war.

One can see pictures taken that day of the dead lying in ditches where they had been rounded up and shot. But in these photographs, the Vietnamese peasants remain the same anonymous victims they have been throughout the war—known only by their body count.

After his conviction, Lt. Calley pointed out that the jury had not heard from one Vietnamese man, woman or child. "I say that's tragic," he told his biographer. "Only the Vietnamese really know it: My Lai, the pain of it."

We decided to tell the story of My Lai the way the Vietnamese experienced it that day. Indeed, to let the children who survived there tell their own story.

TOM FOX RECORDS HIS TRIP TO THE VILLAGE

It was not easy to find these children. Most of the survivors of My Lai are scattered throughout the countryside, either in refugee camps or the homes of relatives. However, I got word from a Vietnamese friend that a few young survivors were still in the refugee camp that had sprung up at the edge of the desolate wilderness of what was once the hamlet of My Lai.

To get to this camp, I flew from Saigon to the provincial capital of Quang Ngai. Then, dressed in brown Mekong delta pajamas, a religious garb, to look as unlike other Americans as possible, I rode the six miles from the airport on the back of a friend's motor scooter. My Lai was still in a relatively insecure area. Only the week before two Vietnamese pacification cadres had been killed on the same road by the Viet Cong, and a German doctor had been captured not much before. A foreigner could not appear alone and unarmed in the area without word quickly spreading. I could stay safely only an hour or two in My Lai.

Many of the survivors in the refugee camp were living in thatched huts not unlike their original ones. But the conditions were mean. Huts were crowded together, each about ten feet from the next. Just beyond the overgrown ruins of what had been My Lai, were the round mounds of the mass graves of the villagers who once lived there.

The peasants were wary of speaking at first. But the children in the camp grew curious when they heard a strange-looking foreigner speaking to them in their language. They seemed to sense I cared about their feelings. When they learned that this book would tell their stories so that the Western world would remember what happened to them at My Lai, they seemed to gain some confidence. Soon they were being encouraged to speak by their parents.

One by one, they told their stories.

HUU

"I was there that morning," thirteen-year-old Do Thi Huu said. "It was early, about eight o'clock. The Americans had been firing into our village for about an hour. We all hid in our shelters under our huts. We were scared. But we knew only a few people ever died in the past when the bombs dropped on the houses. Our shelters were deep and strong.

"Two times before the Americans came into my village. I was afraid of them. They were very big. But they were nice. They did not take any pigs or kill any buffalo. They just looked around the village. And they gave me some candy. So I did not fear them when they came again.

"But that morning was different. They were shouting for us to

come out of our huts: *'Di, di mau! Di, di mau!'* (Hurry up, or Go fast—a basic Vietnamese phrase which American soldiers pick up.)

"My father walked out first. As he stepped outside, one American soldier shot him. Shot him at the door. I cried. My mother screamed. My father fell right in front of our hut. One bullet went into his side, another into his arm. He was lying there bleeding. He did not speak. I cried. But the soldiers grabbed me and took me. I wanted to help my father, but I did not have anything to help him with. They took me and my mother.

"The soldiers told us all to come together in a circle. They called everyone. They told us to stand together. Then they ordered us to sit down."

"Could you understand what they said?"

"They did not speak Vietnamese, but they pushed us down. They wanted us to sit down. I was very frightened. They kept saying 'V.C., V.C.' We told them 'No V.C.'

"They began to take one man out from our circle at a time. Each time they took someone, they shot him, and we cried. I was very afraid. I could not think. I cried, but could not think. They acted slowly. They killed three men, one at a time.

"Then many soldiers knelt down on one knee and fired their guns into us. They shot many, many bullets. There was screaming and crying. Then only the babies cried. I was buried under many people. I cried to myself but did not move. I did not move."

"How many people did the Americans gather together to shoot?"

"I do not know how many. Maybe three hundred, maybe four hundred. Many, many people. All the people they could find."

Huu's mother who was rounded up with her, was killed in the shooting. But Huu did not see her die because the soldiers had pulled them away from each other.

Huu took Tom to the place where everyone was rounded up to be shot. She sat down with her aunt on the spot to show him how the villagers had been forced to sit. Clutching the children of her father's younger brother who died along with his wife in the shooting, she said she dreams about the killings sometimes at night and wakes up crying.

MAI

Nguyen Thi Mai, also thirteen, was in her hut with her parents, brother, sister and grandparents, when she heard the Americans enter the village and begin shooting. She remembers everyone dashing outside and scattering in different directions.

Mai and her father began running out toward the rice paddies. Sometimes her father would pick her up so they could go faster, and other times they would just crawl along the ground together.

They had almost made it to the fields when they realized the Americans had already cordoned off the hamlet. Three soldiers were spread out in front of them about ten meters apart.

"When we saw the soldiers, we stopped running. My father knelt down on his knees and put his hands over his head. I stood in front of him. I wanted to stand between the soldiers and my father. They did not say anything. Then they looked at my father and me. They shot him and walked away.

"A bullet went through my father's chest and blood came out. He was still breathing. I cried and held him in my arms. He looked at me but could not talk. Then he stopped breathing.

"I cried and stayed awhile there with my father. Then I went to look for a place to hide in the fields."

Mai's whole family was killed that morning. Now she lives with some relatives in the camp.

HUYEN

Tran Huyen, thirteen, and his younger sister, Tran Thi Hoang, nine, were the only two in their family besides their grandmother to survive the My Lai massacre. They lost their father and mother, older brother, younger brother and grandfather.

Huyen, like many of the boys in the hamlet that morning, was saved because he was out walking the water buffaloes. He was in the habit of staying away with them for five to seven days at a stretch without returning. He was two days out of My Lai the morning he saw about twenty-five helicopters fly over the hamlet. He was not alarmed because it was common for helicopters to fly over the area.

Not until he was returning to the hamlet the next day did he find out that anything had happened. About a half-mile out he was told by a friend that his parents had been killed and the village burned. He rushed to My Lai, leaving the buffaloes behind.

"I ran into the hamlet. It smelled very much. I saw that every-thing had burned. Most of the people were busy burying their rela-tives. I saw arms and legs and pieces of heads lying around. I ran to my house and saw it was burned down. I lifted the ashes and found my grandfather. Half of him was buried in the shelter. The other half was sticking out. It smelled very bad. I could not under-stand what had happened. Why American soldiers wanted to kill everyone in the village. All the children.

"My mother and father and brothers had already been buried by my relatives when I arrived. I went to their graves. I cried. People told me to go to the hospital to look for my grandmother and sister. I wanted to go, but I didn't because I knew that my father always told me to watch the water buffaloes. I stayed with the buffaloes.

"I still cry when I think of that day. Now my grandmother is old, and I must work to take care of her and my sister."

Huyen helps the farmers plant and harvest the local rice fields. And he watches the water buffaloes.

HOANG

Huyen's nine-year-old sister, Hoang, still remembers the morning of the massacre clearly, although she was only five then.

"I was in our hut with my parents, grandparents and brothers," she said. "The Americans had stopped firing their artillery and we were still inside. I was peeling sweet potatoes so that they could dry in the sun, and we could save them to sell at the market."

Like so many others, she also recalls that the Americans had come to the hamlet twice before without harming them. No one was particularly afraid.

"One American soldier came to our house and moved inside

very quickly. He stopped and looked at us. We did not move. My mother said, 'No. No V.C.'

"First he shot my father with his rifle. Then he shot my older brother. Then he fired again at my younger brother and killed him. Then he shot my grandmother and my grandfather. I saw him killing my family. I looked at him but I do not remember if I cried or screamed. He pointed his gun at my mother. She grabbed me. He shot at us. My mother fell on me. He shot at me and hit my foot. My mother's body was on top of mine. I did not move. It hurt. I cried."

After the soldier left, Hoang saw her grandmother was still moving and groaning. They were the only two alive. They held each other and crawled out of the hut on their knees after they made sure the soldier was out of sight. They managed to get to the rice field where they could see the Americans return to their hut and burn it. They watched the flames devour everything from the fields.

Hoang and her grandmother were taken to the provincial hospital by the other survivors. Eventually they were reunited with her brother and now live together in the refugee camp.

Hoang is shy because of her foot which was deformed by the bullets. Neither she nor her brother go to school because they must work. She helps her grandmother prepare food, and she still gathers sweet potatoes, peels them and dries them in the sun to sell at market—just like she was doing when the troops of Charlie Company arrived that morning.

Epilogue

"When the elephants fight,
the grass gets trampled."

LAOTIAN PROVERB

WE ARE AWARE THAT THERE ARE STILL CHILDREN NOT REPRE-
sented here. The young people of North Vietnam whom we did not
have access to, as well as those of Laos and Cambodia whose lives
are also being disrupted by a war, which now extends throughout
Indochina.

We had hoped that we could end this book on a note of optimism.
That America might truly be "winding down" her involvement in
the conflict with the partial pullout of ground troops, and that a
political settlement might soon be reached at the Paris Peace Talks.

However as this book is finished, in a response to a recent North
Vietnamese offensive, America is renewing massive air strikes over
both the North and the South. The civilian populations continue to
be uprooted and victimized, as the war rages with a ferocity not seen
since Tet of 1968.

Our hope, then, can only be that someday man will learn from
the stories of his victims—such as the children of Vietnam—to
comprehend the horrors he has perpetrated on his fellow man. And
that nations will search for and find alternatives to the strategies of
war in new strategies for peace.

111

Betty Jean Lifton

It seems hard to remember now a time when Vietnam was not in my thoughts. And yet when I first went there as a journalist in 1954, it was not an important place in my life or in my country's. It was a French agony then, not ours.

It was shortly after the Geneva Accords had been signed, dividing Vietnam at the 17th Parallel, that I found myself flying to Hanoi to watch the pullout of the last French troops. The city had an austere, puritanical atmosphere, as if it were already girding itself for the lean years ahead. All that had been French during that eighty-year occupation seemed about to pass with those long convoys of white men, not a few of whom must have loved the city as their own.

The victors at Dien Bien Phu, the troops of Ho Chi Minh, came pouring in from the mountain retreats. They were one of the strongest guerrilla forces in Asia, but they seemed so young and simple as they moved about the decorated streets. But they were not relaxed. "We must not celebrate until we have liberated all of Vietnam," I remember one saying. "For eight years I have lived on rice and salt—rice and salt twice a day—and that is all I will eat until Vietnam is united."

At the time, who of us could imagine how many more years of rice and salt lay ahead.

Saigon, that decadent Southern city, whose gambling casinos and elaborate bordellos were still thriving then, was like the setting of an international drama—the French, Americans and Vietnamese conspiring against each other.

I met at that time some Vietnamese intellectuals and Buddhists who had just formed the Peace Movement, dedicated to working toward elections in 1956, as stipulated in the Geneva agreement. Many of them were already being arrested, and going underground. Years later I learned that they were the original founders of the National Liberation Front, or Viet Cong, as we know it.

My next trip to Vietnam was in the summer of 1967. By then the elections which had never been held had brought their consequences. America had become deeply committed in what we know as the Second Indochina War.

I went this time as a journalist, too. Only now I was also a writer of children's books. I had written about the children of Hiroshima and I wanted to see for myself what was happening to the children of Vietnam. I went through the orphanages, hospitals and shelters in Saigon, and then flew to a few of the provincial hospitals and orphanages in My Tho, Qui Nhon and Danang. There seemed no words to convey the misery of it all, the scope of this tragedy that my country had so unwittingly bungled into in the name of anti-Communism, and now clung to so tenaciously.

When I met Tom Fox back in the States, a journalist who was returning to Vietnam and knew the language well, I suggested we do this book together. We agreed it was important that the young of other countries know about what was happening to the children of Vietnam.

Neither of us was certain then about the exact form the book would take, but Tom was to try to find a cross section of children within the society. I would set the interviews and pictures that he gathered into chapters, and working this way together we would try to tell the story of these children.

Nothing Tom Fox and I do will ever fully tell it. Even this book must ultimately be a failure. But perhaps it will help young people in the Western world to look deeper into political cause and effect than our generation did. To look into the struggles of cultures alien to their own with some empathy.

If our book can help the young reflect on the consequences of war—what it does to nations, to nature, to all of us—then it will have served its purpose. Peace.

BETTY JEAN LIFTON
March 1972

Thomas C. Fox

IT WAS NOT LONG AFTER ARRIVING IN VIETNAM IN 1966 WITH INTER-
national Voluntary Services, a private Peace Corps, that I began to see
how the peasants looked at the war. After a month's intensive language
study, I flew to Central Vietnam and began a fatiguing twenty months
living and working with war refugees.

The Dong Tac refugee camp, until then a sand dune, became the newly
relocated village for nearly three thousand peasants, mostly the old, the
disabled, and bewildered women and children. The young men were dead
or still fighting. They had little food, sometimes only that which they
could beg. The government built them tin shacks into which the peasants
put their few possessions: a tea kettle, cracked dishes, a dirtied picture of
an ancestor. Two miles away in Tuy Hoa city, rice and wheat—United
States AID commodities—grew moldy in government warehouses. Graft
kept the refugees from most of their meager allotments. After six months,
according to government regulations, all AID to them was cut off.

They offered me tea. I was strange to the refugees, but unlike most
others, I showed an interest. But my work grew more and more frustrating.
The medicine I gave them, the clothes and occasional food I could gather
for them, measured as almost nothing in face of their real needs. Diseases
kept spreading. Children starved. They needed much more than I could
offer.

Many spoke quite freely. They were cynical toward the South Vietnamese government. "Only the high people want war. The people below,
in your country and ours, want peace," they said repeatedly, as if to
pardon me for being an American.

They frequently spoke of the United States government. "Why do your
leaders want to make war in Vietnam?" they asked. "Please tell your government about our suffering. Tell them we want the Americans to leave,
the war to end," they would say.

I cannot forget the day a forty-year-old peasant walked near his village the day after it was bombed by American jet planes. In his arms he held the limp, lifeless body of his four-year-old daughter. He looked into my eyes and said, "Tell President Johnson how my daughter died."

It was necessary to speak out publicly against the war. In mid-1967 sixty IVS volunteers, headed by Don Luce, signed an open letter to President Johnson calling for an end to the war. The Tet offensive followed. My work became impossible. I left IVS but stayed in Vietnam to write for the *National Catholic Reporter* and Dispatch News Service International.

Thereafter, I returned to the United States, enrolled in a graduate program at Yale University, and began studying formally about Vietnam. It was at Yale that I met Betty Jean Lifton.

In June 1970 I returned to Vietnam to work on the book and to write for *The New York Times*. That summer I met Hoa, the woman with whom I wanted to share my life. We married the following year. She was a trained social worker who assisted war-injured children. For many months she worked with paraplegic children who had been assisted by the Committee of Responsibility.

It has been nearly five years now that I have lived and worked in Vietnam. During this time few moments have been as painful and fatiguing as those spent with the war's victimized children, some of whom are in this book.

The orphans at the Dieu Quang orphanage, so starved for a simple embrace, dying for lack of affection, begged me to lift them and hold them tightly. At the Children's Convalescent Center I smelled the wretched sweet odors of Mi's burnt flesh as we talked. Mistaking me at first for a doctor, he asked me, "Will I ever be able to use my arm again?" And the children, now living in the cities, tempted by the new life, still talk so often about swimming in rivers and riding water buffaloes, the village life they left behind.

These are sensitive children. Few have been asked to bear so much at such a young age.

THOMAS C. FOX
March 1972

Acknowledgments

We are grateful to the authors and publishers who granted permission to use excerpts from their works in *Children of Vietnam*.

PAGES 2 (bottom), 6, and 56, from Luce, Don, ed., *We Promise One Another,* The Indochina Mobile Education Project, Washington, © 1971.

PAGES 14, 40, and 70 (top), from Ly Qui Chung, ed., *Between Two Fires: The Unheard Voices of Vietnam,* Praeger, New York, © 1970.

PAGES 46 and 51: Reprinted by permission of Dick Hughes from his diary (unpublished).

PAGES 62 (top) and 69, from Huynh Sanh Thuong, trans., *The Tale of Kim Van Kieu,* by Nguyen Du, to be published under the auspices of the Vietnam Studies Coordinating Committee, affiliated with the Association for Asian Studies.

PAGE 2 (top): Lowenfels, Walter, ed., *Where Is Vietnam?,* Double Anchor original paperback, Garden City, New York, © 1967. Reprinted by permission of Larry Jacobs.

PAGE 13 (top): Frank, Anne, *The Diary of a Young Girl,* Doubleday Pocket Book, Garden City, New York, © 1967.

PAGE 13 (bottom): Lifton, Robert J., Kolko, Gabriel, and Falk, Richard, eds., *Crimes of War,* Random House, New York, © 1971.

PAGE 22: Thich Nhat Hanh and Vo-Dinh, *The Cry of Vietnam,* Unicorn Press, Santa Barbara, © 1968. Reprinted by permission of Unicorn Press.

PAGE 32: Erhart, Minh, Phuc, and Balaban, *Vietnamese Folk Poetry,* to be published in 1972 by Carcanet Press, Oxford, England.

PAGE 55: Copyright © 1968, Tradition Music.

PAGE 62 (bottom): Tran Van Dinh, "Why Every American Should Read Kim Van Kieu," reprinted from *Washingtonian* magazine by permission of the author.

PAGE 77: Brelis, Dean, *The Face of South Vietnam,* Houghton Mifflin, Boston, © 1967.

PAGE 83 (top): Luce, Don, and Sommer, John, *Vietnam: The Unheard Voices,* Cornell University Press, Ithaca, © 1969.

PAGE 83 (bottom): Brown, Dee, *Bury My Heart at Wounded Knee,* Holt, Rinehart and Winston, © 1970.

PAGE 91 (top): Hammer, Ellen J., *The Struggle for Indochina, 1940–1955*, Stanford University Press, Stanford, © 1966, page 320. Reprinted by permission of the publishers.

PAGE 91 (middle): Raskin, Marcus, and Fall, Bernard, eds., *The Viet-Nam Reader*, Random House, New York, © 1965.

PAGE 99 (top): Hersh, Seymour, *My Lai 4*, Random House, New York, © 1970.

PAGE 99 (bottom): Horne, Alistair, *The Price of Glory*, St. Martin's, New York, © 1962. Reprinted by permission of St. Martin's Press and Macmillan London and Basingstoke.